Intimacy with God in Singleness

Developing a Relationship with God While Being Single

Deja Smith

WESTBOW
PRESS®
A DIVISION OF THOMAS NELSON
& ZONDERVAN

WestBow Press books may be ordered through booksellers or by contacting:

WestBow Press
A Division of Thomas Nelson & Zondervan
1663 Liberty Drive
Bloomington, IN 47403
www.westbowpress.com
844-714-3454

ISBN: 978-1-5127-1448-7 (sc)
ISBN: 978-1-5127-1449-4 (hc)
ISBN: 978-1-5127-1447-0 (e)

Library of Congress Control Number: 2015916158

Print information available on the last page.

WestBow Press rev. date: 01/19/2023

Contents

Foreword...ix

Introduction...xiii

Chapter 1   Meet Him at the Well..............................1

Chapter 2   Receive His Love 9

Chapter 3   Seek Him 16

Chapter 4   Become Friends.....................................23

Chapter 5   Guard Your Heart..................................30

Chapter 6   Clean House..43

Chapter 7   Develop Your Self-Image 59

Chapter 8   Pursue the Will of God 69

Chapter 9   Be Content...77

Chapter 10 Trust God and Surrender.......................87

References..97

About the Author...99

I dedicate this book to Sydney. God brought us together at the right time. Your zeal and humility have been an inspiration to me and directed my gaze back to Christ on many occasions. I wrote this book for women like us.

To Halima, Jamila and Tinasha, thank you. Thank you for your friendship. Thank you for your honesty. Thank you for your commitment to Christ. I appreciate you all and thank God for your lives.

Mommy, I love you. Thank you for giving me space to spread my wings and fly.

Foreword

By Halima Edge

When I learned of Deja's intentions to write a book about intimacy with God, I immediately desired to write the foreword. I then realized that forewords are normally written by well-known individuals, many of whom are authors of several books and know the individual well.

However, I, (without published books and without popularity) write this foreword as a qualified, primary witness of a young lady who's seek of intimacy with God is pure and worthy to be broadcasted. I'm writing as a witness to the entire process from the beginning to now. I know how the process unfolded, the breakthroughs she experienced and the obedience that led to her victories.

I was a first-hand witness to her journey of intimacy with God, which began around her senior year in college. I watched as the Lord strategically placed her in situations and environments that were conducive for her growth. More importantly, I watched her refuse to succumb to the odds as well as refuse to swim in self-pity. I watched as she rode emotional roller coasters and watched as she later divorced them. I watched as she made bold decisions to protect and further her relationship with God. I watched as she fought to keep her eyes fixed on God, as she purposefully allowed Him to remain number one in her life. I watched as God transformed her from the inside out, where she's now able to help other young women on their journey of purity.

One thing I admire about Deja is her humility and her steadfastness. There were plenty of opportunities to quit and fail, but she always pulled through a conqueror. She went through the process and allowed "endurance [to] have its perfect result, so that [she] may be perfect and complete, lacking in nothing" (James 1:4 NASB).

Did she have moments of defeat? Did she have nights of wanting to quit? Did she have lonesome moments and tearful nights? Sure she did! But did she continue to walk by faith? Yes! In return, she was rewarded with deeper friendship and intimacy with God. My friend, God desires to do the same with you.

I had the opportunity to read this book, and I can truly say that wherever you are in your walk with God, you can benefit from this book. Some who have served the Lord for years may have never experienced true intimacy with God. Some who consider themselves to be intimate with God, will still find encouragement to keep growing in intimacy. Read this book slowly, meditate on the scriptures and allow God to speak to your heart. Journal after each chapter and process how you can add strategy to your life; there are plenty of experiences in which you can connect to and glean from.

This book invites you into Deja's personal journey of intimacy with God and encourages you to desire deeper intimacy in your own life. It is filled with revelation, self-check points and practical things you can do to walk in purity. Many times, while reading this book, I experienced "light-bulb" moments- moments where she perfectly articulated a common struggle that gave insight and was refreshing to my heart. I know it will do the same for you. One more thing; read with expectation and purpose.

Introduction

Be Single

Being single is a special time in a person's life for them to accomplish their dreams and goals and become closer to God. It is a time to develop oneself and make an impact on the lives of others. While being single means not being married or in a relationship with another person, it also reflects the season of life we are in. This time is valuable and precious because it can be used to be single-minded unto God. It is the time to cultivate the things in our lives that are important and will lead to success. It is a time of preparation for more.

If you have decided to read this book, you have probably asked "How can I get closer to God? Where do I start? What does it mean to be intimate with God? How do I get there?" If any of these questions relate to you, this book is for you. Throughout this book I will be sharing ways to become more intimate with God and how I have developed intimacy with Him in my own life.

After a painful breakup, I was left sad, lonely, hurt and empty. I had no idea who God really was or that I could be close to Him. I didn't know how to be single and definitely didn't see the benefits of being single. In time, I learned to use my singleness wisely. God taught me many valuable lessons as a single person and I want to help others who face similar struggles. Having an intimate relationship with God has transformed my life. My desire is for more lives to be touched and transformed through intimacy with God as well.

Early into my relationship with God, I realized that I had a passion for the topic of intimacy. I was fascinated by the fact that we could know and be close to God. Then, as I worked through painful situations in my life, I realized that my nearness to God was what constantly brought me to victory. I originally intended for this book to be solely about intimacy and accessible to both genders. However, as I began to write, I saw that God intended to speak specifically to women who are single.

I will discuss practical things you can do to make room for God to move in your life such as breaking free from past relationships and hurts, making Jesus the Lord of every area of your life and pursuing God's will. It is my prayer that this book, with the help of the Holy Spirit, will refresh your spirit and empower you to prosper as a single woman.

I'm writing this book in the process of life. I am not married and don't know when or how it will happen, but I know God. I have tasted and seen that the Lord is good. I can boldly say that where I am in my relationship with God, few people ever get to. Not because they aren't able, but because they are not willing. I believe that if you are reading this book, you will come into that place of intimacy with God. You will know Him more deeply than you ever have. You will encounter God in the deeper place.

In 1 Corinthians 7, Paul gives advice on marriage and singleness. Paul has not received any direct commands from God regarding singleness so he is sharing his advice and wisdom. In verse 25 he says "Now regarding your question about the young women who are not yet married, I do not have a command from the Lord for them. But the Lord in His mercy has given me wisdom that can be trusted, and I will share it with you. Because of the present crisis, I think it is best to remain as you are." (1 Cor. 7:25-26 New Living Translation).

One interpretation refers to the "present crisis" as the pressures of life. There are so many pressures that we all face and that can lead us away from God. When we are married we have more responsibility and pressure, so Paul is saying it is good if we don't have any added stress. He goes on to say "If you have a wife, do not seek to end the marriage. If you do not have a wife, do not seek to get married. But if you do get married, it is not a sin. And if a young woman gets married, it is not a sin. However, those who get married at this time will have troubles, and I am trying to spare you those problems." (1 Cor. 7:27-28 NLT).

I do not want you to take this scripture negatively. Paul clearly says that being married is not a sin. He is simply saying that being single is a blessing because you have less worries and concerns. Being married is a blessing that brings a greater amount of responsibility to your daily life. Both seasons bring something different to the table. In both seasons you connect with the Lord in a way that you can't fully do in the other. I am just focusing on singleness and its benefits in this book.

1 Corinthians 7:32-35 (NLT) says "I want you to be free from the concerns of this life. An unmarried man can spend his time doing the Lord's work and thinking how to please him. But a married man has to think about his earthly responsibilities and how to please his wife. His interests are divided. In the same way, a woman who is no longer married or has never

been married can be devoted to the Lord and holy in body and in spirit. But a married woman has to think about her earthly responsibilities and how to please her husband. I am saying this for your benefit, not to place restrictions on you. I want you to do whatever will help you serve the Lord best, with as few distractions as possible."

With that being said, I view being single as an opportunity to:

- Spend time doing the Lord's work
- Focus on how to please God
- Be fully devoted to God
- Be holy and set apart
- Have few distractions
- Develop an intimate relationship with God

Have you ever wondered what you should focus on when you are single? I believe that while you are single you should be developing trust in God and doing good. The bible says to "trust in the Lord and do good." (Psalm 37:3 New King James Version). Learn to cast your care on Him. Trust God and do what He says. Be obedient to what He asks of you. Whether it is to serve in a particular ministry or help someone in need or sow a particular seed. Just trust what He says and do it!

The very next verse reads "Delight yourself also in the Lord and He shall give you the desires of your heart." (Psalm 37:4 NKJV). This sounds awesome but how can we really "delight" ourselves in the Lord? How can we get to the place where we are enjoying God? It comes from making Him a priority in our lives. God wants us to enjoy Him and focus on Him and not our relational status. Once we get to that place He gives us the very things that we wanted.

While you are single you don't have to worry about anyone else's well-being besides your own. Your time is your own and you can use it to please God and do work for his kingdom. You can join and teach bible study groups, volunteer at shelters and go on mission trips. You can focus on what God is doing in your life and the lives of others. As a single person, you can develop kingdom friendships with other believers. Use this time to be a blessing to people around you and help God transform this world.

Being single is the perfect time to develop your relationship with God and fall in love with Him. You can be faithful to Him and dedicated to His word. You can develop a new understanding and revelation of the Word of God. You can become passionate about the things of God. The season of singleness is a time to be set apart and pure. You can work with God to be free from all entanglements and ungodly soul ties. The possibilities are limitless!

Singleness is a time of few distractions. If you don't have a husband you don't have to be worried about how to please him. You don't have to cook for another person and worry about where they are and what they are doing. There is so much time and freedom available. I am not saying those things are bad. Having a husband is a blessing from God. I am saying that it is a blessing from God to be free and enjoy it. Ecclesiastes 3:12 (NLT) says "So I concluded there is nothing better than to be happy and enjoy ourselves as long as we can".

Be single and enjoy it. This is the time for you to get your personal life in order. Get a picture and vision for your life and work with God to see it come to pass. If there is something you don't want to bring into your marriage or pass on to your kids, you can change it now! Decide what habits you want to develop in your life and put them in place.

I pray that through reading this book you will receive revelation from God about your specific situation. I believe you will also receive a heavenly perspective about singleness. I pray that your eyes and your heart will become open to God and that you will appreciate this season and its many benefits. I also pray that you will develop an intimate relationship with God. A relationship where there is open communication, mutual love and trust. A relationship where you are able to hear from God clearly and encounter the love He has for you.

Developing an intimate relationship with God while you are single is one of the best investments you can make in your life. Getting to know who Jesus is and how much He loves you will establish a foundation from which you will build your life. No matter what God has planned, you can enjoy the ride because you are in an intimate relationship with Him.

Chapter 1

Meet Him at the Well

Everything you have been searching and longing
for is found in Jesus.

The following revelation of the story of the "Woman at the Well" is a message from the heart of God to you. I pray that the eyes of your understanding will be enlightened and that you will encounter the presence of God. Even if the story of the woman at the well in John 4 is very familiar and you have heard it several times, I believe that you will receive new insight and wisdom from this story. If you are unfamiliar with this passage then I recommend that you read John 4:1-42 before continuing this chapter.

One Sunday morning, my pastor was teaching from John 4 on the conversation between the woman at the well and Jesus. All of a sudden, I heard a woman behind me weeping. I thought to myself, maybe she's been through some hard times with men and some other judgmental thoughts until I heard God say, "You were the Samaritan Woman." I looked around in utter confusion. I thought, "I haven't been with five men, I didn't have five husbands, how could I possibly be like her?"

As I had these thoughts, my pastor then said, "Men were her source." My eyes opened wide and my heart started to beat faster. Although I hadn't been intimate with five men, men too were my source. Before I gave my life to Christ, I was constantly in a relationship. If I didn't have a boyfriend, then I was dating someone. I always felt that I had to be in a relationship. I felt like less of a person if I didn't have an emotional attachment to a man, even if I didn't really like him. However, this meant that something other than God was always filling my void for God. I allowed relationships to take up space that I should have given to God. So, I went home and began to study John 4 to figure out what God was trying to show me.

The first thing God showed me about the woman's encounter with Jesus was that the timing was strategic. John

4:4 (NKJV) says "But He needed to go through Samaria." Jesus had a purpose and a plan. He knew exactly what would happen when He went there. While He was at the well, the disciples were away getting something to eat. Jesus encountered the woman at the well when she was alone (single). They shared an intimate exchange. No one else was around to distract them. No friends, no family, no boyfriend, no husband, no kids. Just her and Jesus.

Jesus encountered her in a place of singleness, a place of intimacy. God is also looking for an intimate exchange with you in your singleness. This is exactly what He wants to do with you. While you are single, He desires to encounter you; He desires to be intimate with you. This book is your prophetic well. You may not be sitting at a well with Jesus in the physical realm, but in the spiritual realm He is looking at you saying just what He said in John 4:7 (NKJV), "Give me a drink." This is an invitation to begin anew with Him. Jesus wants you to drink from Him today. He wants you to know who He is and He wants you to experience His love and freedom.

Jesus knew what the outcome of the conversation with the woman at the well would be. He knew that she wasn't happy with her life and that He had a better way for her to live. You may be unhappy with your life right now. Maybe you have had many relationships and the one you are in now is not fulfilling. Maybe you are lonely and looking for something, but you don't know what it is. If so, then you can relate to this woman.

I was in a relationship with a guy for six years. He was my "first love" and the one I thought I would marry. Towards the end of the relationship, I was very unhappy. We were dating long distance and I knew that he was cheating on me. I was depressed and cried every day. I had no peace and no joy, yet

I stayed in the relationship. I knew in my heart that I should leave, but I saw no other option but to stay in it. Like this woman, I was at the well getting water that would make me "thirst again."

If you are in an unhealthy relationship with someone, then you are also getting water that will make you thirst again. It's a temporary satisfaction. You will always have to go back to that "source" because the love and happiness you feel in those brief moments of pleasure always wear off; they never last. When you make a human your source it will always leave you feeling empty. For example, even though we decided to end the relationship, we were still sexually involved. I was thirsty and needed some water to drink. I needed something to fill me up and make me feel loved. However, this water made me thirst again and again.

So, Jesus continues to say to this woman in John 4:14 (NKJV), "whoever drinks of the water that I shall give him will never thirst." Imagine her excitement! It was probably as if someone had offered her a million dollars. "Sir, give me this water that I may not thirst, nor come here to draw." (John 4:15 NKJV) We can look at this in the natural way, but I want to examine it from a spiritual perspective.

This woman's soul was thirsty, she was longing for God. That is because God is the only one who can satisfy your soul. We were created to worship God, serve God and be loved by God. When we let something else take His place, it never works. She was filling her soul with men because she was lacking a relationship with God. When Jesus offered her living water her spirit and her soul were jumping for joy. There is always a deeper meaning behind what Jesus says. The water He offered was actually Himself-the only thing that could satisfy her soul. That same water is available to every thirsty soul in the world today.

As I was studying this chapter, I had a conversation with God about why men were her source. How did she get to that place? How did I get to the place where men were my source? God revealed to me that one of the reasons was because of my relationship with my father. Although I didn't have a bad relationship with my father, I never had an intimate relationship with him. I never got to sit in his lap or rest on his shoulders. My father spent some time in prison in my early years and we had to develop our relationship when he returned home. I was rebellious towards him for a while and didn't feel connected to him. He also was emotionally distant because he wasn't raised in a loving and affectionate home.

Therefore, I unknowingly sought out attention and affection from men. I loved the attention and it gave me a sense of self-worth. I didn't know who I was and I certainly didn't know my value. Having someone to talk to and tell me I was beautiful was gratifying. I also didn't know the unconditional love of Jesus, so I filled my emotional needs with men. All I really wanted was to feel accepted and loved. If the woman at the well had an upbringing similar to mine, I can totally understand how she found herself in that position.

Many women suffer from being fatherless. They seek to fill the void of their father in other men, and it can result in long-lasting devastation on their souls. If you can relate to this situation, then I pray that God would fill every void in your heart. He is the father to the fatherless (Psalm 68:5 NKJV). No matter what has happened in your life between you and your father, God is able to give you beauty for ashes and heal any pain you have from that relationship.

We can see this as the chapter continues. Now that Jesus had her attention, it was time to deal with the hindrances. In John 4:16 (NKJV), He asked the woman to get her husband. Her soul wanted to get closer to God, but there was something that could have hindered her decision if she didn't make the right choice. Once you have an encounter with Jesus, there is always a choice to be made. She could have chosen to go back to the temporary satisfaction of a man or turn to the everlasting satisfaction of Jesus. The Samaritan woman made the right choice. She said "I have no husband."

After I gave my life to Christ and had my personal encounter with God, I knew I was going to have to give up my relationship. I could have refused and held on to the relationship, but instead I faced the truth. The man I was dating was not my husband. The woman at the well did the same thing. She acknowledged that she was in a relationship that she shouldn't be in and was honest with God. In order to be closer to God, we have to be willing to be honest about our mess. We have to be willing to confess our sins so that Jesus can free us from them.

The woman understood that there was a better life available to her. In John 4:25 (NKJV) she says, "I know that the Messiah is coming. When He comes He will tell us all things." She had faith that there was a better way of life. In my own desperate situation, I cried out to God. I was totally unhappy with my life and I knew that God was real. I knew that there was a place of intimacy I could experience. I believed that there was a God who loved me and could turn my life around. He can do the same for you too!

In John 4:26 (NKJV), Jesus reveals that He is the Messiah, the Savior. He is the one she was looking for. He is the one who can tell her all things. He is the one who can give her the everlasting water. He is everything she needs. Jesus is also everything you need. Everything you have been searching and longing for is found in Jesus. He is your Messiah.

When the disciples came back it was time for the woman to make her exit. John 4:28 (NKJV) says that the woman left her water pot. I love this because it shows that she made a concrete decision. I believe that the water pot symbolizes her agenda. It was what she was doing with her life before she encountered God. It represents her plan for her life. The moment she walked away from the water pot, she decided not to take her baggage with her. She left her association with her old life at the well. She left her water pot with Jesus at the place where she encountered Him.

Once this woman became free, she went out and told others about Jesus. She had a new vision for her life. She was going to tell others about this encounter and encourage them to have an encounter of their own. That is what happened to me, and I believe Jesus desires the same for you. He wants you to be free from unhealthy relationships and anything else that would take His place in your life. He wants to encounter you so that you can tell others about Him. He wants you to have a new perspective on life. 1 John 5:21(AMP) says "Little children (believers, dear ones), guard yourselves from idols- [false teachings, moral compromises, and anything that would take God's place in your heart]."

I believe that Jesus will realign you during your time of singleness just like He did with this woman. You have a purpose to fulfill. There are people that you are called to impact. Take this time of singleness to make God your source and discover His plan for your life. Decide to follow Him no matter the cost.

Think about it...

- How can you relate to the Samaritan Woman?
- How has your relationship with your father impacted your relationship with men?
- In the past, what have you used to fill God's place in your heart?
- How does this story inspire you to be closer to God?

Prayer

Jesus, I thank you for desiring to encounter me. I pray that you will come closer to me than ever before. Jesus, when I don't feel worthy of your love and pursuit I pray that you will open my eyes to the truth. I chose to turn to you so that you may satisfy me. I pray that you will be the source of my life. Please help me to release the things that I have used to fill me. Please help me to heal from past hurts. You know everything about me and you only want what's best for me. I pray that you will show me your purpose and plan for my life and help me to walk in it.

Chapter 2

Receive His Love

Receiving God's love is a key to unlocking greater levels of intimacy with Him.

An important aspect of developing an intimate relationship with God is accepting His love for you. The first step in doing so is acknowledging Jesus' sacrifice for you. If you are a follower of Christ, then you believe and have confessed that Jesus died to pay the price for your sin. Jesus laid down His life because He loved you and wanted you to be a part of God's kingdom. John 3:16 (NIV) reads "For God so loved the world that he gave his one and only Son, that whoever believes in him shall not perish but have eternal life." This is the foundation of your relationship with Him and the greatest gift you could ever receive.

Having a revelation of God's love for you changes everything. When you know how much He loves you, you can't stay the same. As time goes on, your love for Him will only grow deeper. Nothing compares to God's love and nothing has the power to transform like His love. As you seek to develop an intimate relationship with Him, I pray that "you have the power to understand, as all God's people should, how wide, how long, how high, and how deep his love is. May you experience the love of Christ, though it is too great to understand fully. Then you will be made complete with all the fullness of life and power that comes from God." (Ephesians 3:18-19 NLT)

One of the ways that you can receive God's love is by learning more about who He is. You can do this by reading scriptures about His attributes. You can read stories in the bible of how He has shown up in the lives of others and done what only He could. Reading what the bible says about God will help to paint a clear picture of His character. Hearing stories about what He has done for others will help you see who He really is. When you read verses where God speaks to people, I encourage you to take some time to think about what aspects of God's character you can discover.

Psalm 103 is a great chapter to read and meditate on because it speaks to God's nature. Psalm 103:8-13 (NLT) says, "The Lord is compassionate and merciful, slow to get angry and filled with unfailing love. He will not constantly accuse us, nor remain angry forever. He does not punish us for all our sins; he does not deal harshly with us, as we deserve. For his unfailing love toward those who fear him is as great as the height of the heavens above the earth. He has removed our sins as far from us as the east is from the west. The Lord is like a father to his children, tender and compassionate to those who fear him."

To me, these scriptures reveal how God feels about us and how He treats us. He is compassionate, kind, loving, patient, forgiving and merciful. Knowing these attributes will help you to see the truth about God. Since He has those traits, you can believe that He will treat you in a way that lines up with His personality. He will be patient with you, forgive you, be kind and loving towards you. You will desire to be closer to Him when you know more about Him.

While you are drawing closer to God, it is important to address fears, negative mindsets and lies you believe about God. These things can create filters that misrepresent Him and keep you from seeing Him clearly. Eliminating those filters won't happen overnight but they will disintegrate as you learn more about God and experience His love for yourself. It is easier to receive His love when you have a positive view of God and believe the truth about Him.

One lie that I believed about God was that He didn't love me or want to have a relationship with me because of my sin. I struggled to believe that God really loved me because I felt unworthy of His love and acceptance. Like the woman at the well, I was shocked that God was even interested in speaking with me. I felt disqualified from receiving love because I believed that God would only love me if I did everything He wanted me to do. I didn't know that God loved me regardless of my actions. As time went on, I discovered that I believed this lie as a result of situations from my childhood.

Before I understood how much God loves me, if I made a mistake I felt that God was mad at me and that made me afraid to talk to Him. Growing up, there were times when my father would get upset with me and stop talking to me if I did something he didn't like. So, I tried my best to make him and everyone else happy so that I wouldn't lose their love and acceptance. I thought that if I did what other people wanted me to do, I would be accepted by them. If I didn't do what they wanted or expected of me, I thought they would reject me.

As a result of my life experiences, I learned that if you disappoint someone they stop expressing love to you. I learned that it is okay to withhold from people when they upset you. These mindsets impacted how I viewed God. I couldn't receive His love because I thought He was disappointed and upset with me. I believed that He would avoid me because I was a sinner and wasn't living up to His standards. These wrong beliefs kept me from developing an intimate relationship with God.

Let me be clear that God does not view sin lightly. He cares about what we do. I just had to learn that because I did something bad, it didn't mean that God would write me off. If I was being disobedient or in habitual sin, He wasn't pleased but He still loved me. The same is true for you. Your actions don't make God stop loving you. He doesn't give His love based on conditions. There are no rules for receiving His love and acceptance.

I now know the unconditional love of my Heavenly Father. God is perfect and He is a good father. He doesn't stop talking to me just because I did something He didn't like. He won't lash out at me in anger because I upset Him. I don't have to walk on eggshells and wait for His anger to subside before I get in His presence again. He will continue to provide and care for me, even when I make mistakes. He loves me unconditionally! God desires for all of us to experience His love that comes without conditions.

Receiving God's love is a process. It's not a destination you arrive at. It is a journey with many stops along the way. Sometimes bad things happen in life and they make you question God's love. I pray that you will allow Him to heal any place in you that makes it difficult to receive His love. This may look like confronting issues from your childhood, going to therapy and having hard conversations with the Lord. As you heal, you will experience more of God's love for you.

Are there any fears you have of God? (Not counting a reverential fear of Him). Are you afraid that He will disappoint you or forget you? Are you afraid He won't protect you? What lies might you be believing about Him? Do you think He doesn't want to communicate with you? Or that He doesn't care about your needs? I would like you to set aside time to write out or journal some of the obstacles you face when it comes to receiving God's love. Don't hold your true feelings back. Then pray and ask Him to speak to you about what you wrote.

Another step to receiving God's love is realizing that you can't understand it. He doesn't love like a human because He is not human. He is God. He doesn't love the way we are used to. He doesn't see things the way we do. Part of receiving God's love is embracing mystery. It's accepting the fact that it doesn't make sense. His love for us is so deep and encompassing that it surpasses what we can comprehend.

Ephesians 1:4-5 (NLT) reads "Even before he made the world, God loved us and chose us in Christ to be holy and without fault in his eyes. God decided in advance to adopt us into his own family by bringing us to himself through Jesus Christ. This is what he wanted to do, and it gave him great pleasure." Before God created the world, He loved you. Before you were born, He chose you. Before you messed up, He had a plan for Jesus to make you holy.

Receiving God's love is a key to unlocking greater levels of intimacy with Him. I pray that you will have a deeper understanding of His love for you. His love is truly inexhaustible and you will encounter more of it in each season of your relationship with Him.

Think about it…

Here are some scriptures about God's love that
you can read when you need reminding.

Luke 12:7 (NLT) "And the very hairs on your
head are all numbered. So, don't be afraid; you
are more valuable to God than a whole flock of
sparrows."

1 John 3:1 (NLT) See how very much our Father loves us, for he calls us his children, and that is what we are!

Romans 5:8 (NIV) But God demonstrates his own love for us in this: While we were still sinners, Christ died for us.

Romans 8:38-39 (NLT) And I am convinced that nothing can ever separate us from God's love. Neither death nor life, neither angels nor demons, neither our fears for today nor our worries about tomorrow—not even the powers of hell can separate us from God's love. No power in the sky above or in the earth below— indeed, nothing in all creation will ever be able to separate us from the love of God that is revealed in Christ Jesus our Lord.

Prayer

Father God, I thank you for loving me. You have always loved me and you will always love me no matter what. I pray for a greater understanding of your love. Help me to believe without a doubt that I am deeply loved by you. Please help me to see the truth of who you are and dispel any lies that I have believed about your character. Help me to be open to receive your love.

Chapter 3

Seek Him

Those who really want to find God will.

Seeking God is vital to your level of intimacy with Him. In this busy world, many things can distract us from what is really important. It requires constant effort to set aside time to be with God and stay connected to Him. We may go through seasons of life where we are busier than others, but it is our job to make sure our priorities are in order. As you seek to be closer to God, I pray that you will be focused and diligent in your pursuit of Him. You can rest in knowing that when you seek Him you will find Him. (Jeremiah 29:13)

In addition, we have to check our motives for spending time with God. It's easy to seek Him out when we are in need or have troubles. But we shouldn't only spend time with God because we need Him to do something for us. Matthew 6:33 says "But seek first the kingdom of God and His righteousness, and all these things shall be added to you." God knows what you need and will take care of you. Just be with Him.

As we seek to make God a priority in our lives, we have to be sure to read the Bible and spend time in worship daily. These two things are essential to victory. When I first began my relationship with God I knew I had to change my routine in order to see any growth. I used to talk on the phone with my boyfriend every day at 9:00 PM. That was our time to discuss our lives and our relationship. Once that relationship ended and I became a Christian, I replaced that time with reading the Bible and worshiping God.

Each day at 9:00 PM, I would shut everything down and get alone with God. I turned off the television, and logged off of social media. I put my phone away so that it wouldn't be a distraction. I gave God the same level of attention and focus that I would give someone who was very important to me and whose relationship I highly valued.

That is how I developed my relationship with God. That is how we became intimate. As a result of me pursuing Him in this daily personal time we became closer. As I read the Bible, I began to hear His voice more clearly. As I worshiped Him with my whole heart, free from distractions, I experienced His love for me. After a while it wasn't hard to spend time with God. In fact, I really wanted to because I knew I needed to. You see, the bigger God becomes in your life, the more you realize just how much you need Him.

Even Jesus needed to set aside time to spend with the Father. There are many examples in scripture of times where Jesus separated himself from crowds and the disciples to pray and be alone. Mark 1:35 (NIV) says "Very early in the morning, while it was still dark, Jesus got up, left the house and went off to a solitary place, where he prayed." Matthew 14:23 (NLT) reads "After sending them home, he went up into the hills by himself to pray. Night fell while he was there alone." He made space in His life to seek the Father, it was a priority He established for Himself.

If Jesus had this measure of discipline to pursue the Father then we should as well. It will take intentionality to be solitary. You may have to schedule your time in your calendar or plan your week with more thoughtfulness. We have many responsibilities that we can't ignore but we must do what's necessary to carve out space to be alone with God. Our time with Him keeps us aligned to His will. That is where we get filled and renewed.

God wants us to pursue Him. Psalm 14:2 (NKJV) says that "The Lord looks down from heaven upon the children of men, to see if there are any who understand, who seek God." God is looking for people who seek Him. He desires children that are after His heart and desire Him in return. David wrote in Psalm 27:8 (NKJV) "When You said, 'Seek My face,' my heart said to You, 'Your face, Lord, I will seek'." God wants to be with us, so may we respond like David as well.

King David is an awesome example of a person who sought God. In Psalm 27 we get a glimpse of his relationship with God. Psalm 27:4 (NKJV) says "One thing I have desired of the Lord, that will I seek: That I may dwell in the house of the Lord all the days of my life, to behold the beauty of the Lord and to inquire in His temple." David is saying there is only one thing that I want from God, only one thing that I am striving after. That one thing is intimacy. It's a relationship with God. He desired to be connected to God for his entire life.

When we are pursuing God, it will be reflected in how we spend our time and the places we frequent. Psalm 26:8 (NKJV) states "I love your sanctuary, Lord, the place where your glorious presence dwells." How often do you go to church, homegroup or Christian events? God's presence isn't only at those places but it is important to put yourself in places where He is. Be like David, wherever the presence of God is that's where you should desire to be.

I absolutely love Psalm 63. It is one of my favorite chapters in the bible. Verse 1 says: "O GOD, You are my God; Early I will seek You; My soul thirsts for You; My flesh longs for You in a dry and thirsty land where there is no water." (Psalm 63:1 NKJV) David was desperate for God and wanted only Him. The level of intimacy that David had can inspire and encourage us all to seek God. The part of this verse that I want to discuss is "early I will seek You". What does your morning routine look like?

I love to start my day with God. I try to connect with Him as soon as I wake up and give Him my attention. Psalm 5:3 (AMP) reads "In the morning, O LORD, You will hear my voice; In the morning I will prepare [a prayer and a sacrifice] for You and watch *and* wait [for You to speak to my heart]." Let God be the first thing on your mind in the morning. Let Him be the first one you talk to everyday. Seek God in the morning and it will make you more aware of Him throughout the day.

Your time with God doesn't have to be in the morning. For some people mornings may work best because you have a pocket of time before work or school. For others it may be at night before bed. It can be during your lunch break at work. It truly doesn't matter when you find time, all that matters is that you do. Developing an intimate relationship with God requires time. It's more about the quality than the quantity. Ten minutes of worship and praise can feel more impactful than an hour spent distracted and not fully present to God's voice.

During your time with God, you can read the bible, pray, worship, listen to teachings and more. There is no rule book or steps you must follow. Flow with God and do what feels natural. Ask Him what He would like to do. Sometimes, God will instruct me to write in my journal. I don't know why at first and then I find myself writing out my true emotions and God steps in to comfort me. Other times, He leads me to a story in the bible or a specific scripture. The point is to be open to what God wants to do during your time with Him.

In order to grow deeper in intimacy, I learned to use my imagination to encounter God. When I first began using my imagination to encounter God, I would turn on worship music and sit and imagine myself in a field of flowers. Once I got a clear picture in my mind, I would picture Jesus standing next to me. Eventually, it became easier because I had been to that place in my mind so often. From there I would let my imagination run wild and let Jesus take me wherever He wanted to.

I had to learn to be more childlike in order to engage with God this way. In Matthew 18:3 Jesus said "Truly I tell you, unless you change and become like little children, you will never enter the kingdom of heaven." Children aren't afraid to use their imaginations and they do so often. This may sound strange but it has brought me closer to Him. Jesus knows how to speak to you. He knows what you like and how to communicate with you in a way that you understand. He wants to take you places and show you things to come, so put yourself in a place to receive.

I pray that in your pursuit of God, you would grow to a place where you genuinely desire to be with Him. I pray that you would find joy and peace in His presence and rest for your soul. I pray that you would do whatever is necessary to go after Him. I pray that you would develop a greater hunger for God and discipline to quiet yourself. When you seek God just because you want to spend time with Him then you will know you have reached a greater level of intimacy.

Think about it…

- How have you shown God that you are seeking Him?
- What is one thing you can do to seek Him more?
- How can you change your routine/schedule to seek God?

Prayer

God, I desire to make you a priority in my life. As I set aside time to be with you, help me to be disciplined in my pursuit of you. Show me how I can make room for you in my daily schedule and may I be willing to adjust to make it happen. Please help me not to be easily distracted and to enjoy my time with you. I pray that you would give me a heart that desires to spend time with you. I pray that we will grow closer and more intimate during our time together.

Chapter 4

Become Friends

Every meaningful relationship we have in life
is based on a great friendship.

God desires to have a real relationship with you. He wants to spend time together. He wants you to know His thoughts and plans and He wants to know yours. He wants to talk to you about the good and the bad. He wants to have a true friendship with you. This chapter is focused on how we can use this season of singleness to develop a solid friendship with God.

In your season of singleness, it is imperative that you learn how to be friends with God. Every meaningful relationship we have in life is based on a great friendship. The level of intimacy you develop with Him in secret will carry over into every area of your life. By developing a strong foundation with Him now, you are setting yourself up for success in the future.

Being a friend of God will change your life. You will fall deeper in love with Him. You will learn about Him and about yourself. You'll be satisfied and He will meet your needs in the deepest and most blessed ways. Your friendship with God should be the foundation of your life. No other relationship or friendship should come before your friendship with God.

"Your eyes saw my substance, being yet unformed. And in your book they were all written, the days fashioned before me, when as yet there were none of them." (Psalm 139:16 NKJV) This scripture is revelatory to me because it's saying that before we were born, God already knew every single detail of our lives. All our days were written out before we even got here. This shows us that we were in the heart of God before we were created.

The next verse says "How precious also are Your thoughts to me O God! How great is the sum of them! If I should count them, they would be more in number than the sand; When I awake, I am still with you." (Psalm 139:17 NKJV) This scripture says that His thoughts for us outnumber the grains of sand! It's impossible to understand the sheer quantity of thoughts God must have about us. The King of Glory thinks about us more than we can comprehend. Knowing how much God thinks about us, helps us to have a greater awareness of His presence.

This scripture is an invitation to friendship and intimacy with God. He knows you better than anyone ever could. Since He is always thinking about you, you can be assured that He always wants to talk to you. Plus, He is always available. I love the fact that Jesus can always talk to us. We don't have to wait for Him to get out of a meeting or call back after work. He is always able to talk. He is always ready and waiting to speak with you. Jesus is the best possible friend to have.

Think about a close friendship you have and how much time you spend with that person. I'm sure that the more time you have spent with that person the more like them you have become. You may have started to talk like them, or dress like them because you are around them all the time. Well it's the same with God. He is always with you and the more time you spend with Him on purpose, the more like Him you will become.

It's easy to know a person, see them often and still remain an acquaintance. Think of a co-worker that you see all the time but know nothing about. What makes the difference in the relationship is quality time spent. God doesn't want to be an acquaintance that you only see on Sundays. He wants to be a friend that you spend time with daily.

Developing a friendship with the Lord will allow you to navigate life in a healthier and easier way. Becoming friends with Jesus and learning to lean on Him will protect you from becoming codependent on any other person or getting yourself into unnecessary situations because you are lonely. I say this from experience. If I would have spent more time becoming a better friend to Jesus, then I could have spared myself and others from heartache.

When I look back over my life and reflect on some of the situations I found myself in, I realized that what I was truly looking for was companionship. I just wanted someone to spend time with. Someone to feel close to and wanted by. I didn't fully understand that Jesus was capable of being my friend in this way. I didn't know I could talk to Him, hear from Him and enjoy Him just like I would a friend.

If you are still learning how to hear from God, I want to say that there is more than one way to communicate with God. Scripture is the main way through which God speaks. However, some people grow to hear Him speak in a "still small voice". (1 Kings 19:11-13 NKJV). Some people see pictures in their mind or have dreams. Some people have strong feelings or an overwhelming sense of knowing inside of them. The beauty of this journey is that you get to learn how to communicate with God in a way that works for you. Don't be discouraged if you don't get anything right away. Have faith that God can and will speak to you.

He desires to give you insight and guidance and simply to love you. Exodus 33:11 (NKJV) reads "the Lord spoke to Moses face to face, as a man speaks to a friend." Moses isn't the only person that can talk to God, you can too. This is proof that God is willing and able to be our friend. Not only is He the Creator of the world, He is also a friend.

There are many ways that we can build a friendship with God. They are similar to how we develop friendships with people. To develop a friendship, you must express yourself. It is important to talk to your friend about the good and bad things of life. You can tell them your secrets and laugh at each other's jokes. This is what God wants to do with you. Psalm 25:14 (NKJV) says "The secret of the Lord is with those who fear Him". We can be honest with Him and tell Him everything because He already knows anyway. But we can also learn from Him the secrets that He wants to share with us.

God also loves to laugh. He has created us in His image and likeness, so naturally we enjoy laughter as well. Job 8:21 (NKJV) says "He will fill your mouth with laughing, and your lips with rejoicing". God knows what will make you laugh because He created you. There have been many times where I was feeling down and God showed me a picture in my mind of something very silly that made me laugh. This made me connect to Him and realize that He isn't serious all the time.

Another way to develop a friendship with someone is to do things with that person. In a similar fashion, you can invite God into everything you do. When you are cooking or shopping, talk to Him. Ask Him for advice on what you should wear and wait for His answer. Talk to Him about your day when you are eating dinner. Seek His opinion about how to handle a difficult situation. It may be weird at first but the more you do it, the easier it becomes.

He knows where you are and what you are up to at all times. He knows everything you do because He is acquainted with all your ways. (Psalm 139:3 NKJV) Just talk to Him like you would a friend. Don't try to use big fancy words to impress Him. Be real with Him and you will soon find that He is the best friend you could ever have.

To be a friend of God, we have to become more like Him. God is holy and good and in order to maintain a relationship with

Him, we must pursue what is holy and good. It is not possible for us to live evil, sinful lives and have a close relationship with God. Psalm 3:31-32 (NLT) says "Don't envy violent people or copy their ways. Such wicked people are detestable to the Lord but He offers His friendship to the godly." When our lives are holy and pure we can come closer to God. The more undefiled we become, the deeper, more intimate fellowship we can have with Jesus.

It is important to note that Jesus cares about how we treat other people. He values every life and sees no one as insignificant. He cares about how good of a friend you are to others. Hebrews 12:14 (NKJV) says "Pursue peace with all people, and holiness, without which no one will see the Lord: looking carefully lest anyone fall short of the grace of God; lest any root of bitterness springing up cause trouble, and by this many become defiled."

Unforgiveness is a serious issue because as the scripture just mentioned, it will cause you to become bitter. When you don't have peace with people, then you will not be able to see the Lord clearly. Be careful how you treat other people and be quick to forgive every offense. How you treat others should reflect your relationship with God.

Another way we can have a closer friendship with Jesus is by being truthful with Him. Psalm 51:6 (NKJV) says "You desire truth in the inward parts." God wants us to be loyal and faithful and sincere with Him. He already knows it all but we have to be willing to tell the truth. Be willing to tell the truth about your feelings and desires, the truth about your fears and worries and the truth about who He is to you.

You can tell Him, "God I know I don't know you very well but I want to know you more. We may not be close friends now, but I want to be best friends. Thank you for offering your friendship to me." No matter where you are in your friendship with God, you can be closer. If you aren't where you want to be then there is no time like the present to make a change.

1 John 3:20 (NLT) says "Even if we feel guilty, God is greater than our feelings, and He knows everything." God is greater than any thought or emotion you may have. You can be straightforward with Him and tell Him how you feel. This is how you develop intimacy and friendship with God.

Think about it...

- How does it make you feel to know that God's thoughts for you outnumber the grains of sand?
- How often do you talk to Jesus?
- What can you do to be a better friend to God?

Prayer

God, I thank you for your friendship. Thank you for giving me access to you. Lord, I pray that our friendship will be deeper and more intimate. Show me how I can allow you into more areas of my life. Help me to become more aware of you throughout my day. I want to have clear communication with you. Like Moses, I want to speak to you face to face. Help me to be a better friend to you. I pray that I will learn more about you and have a solid friendship with you.

Chapter 5

Guard Your Heart

You have the power to keep your heart pure.

Guarding your heart is very important to the development of your relationship with God and your quality of life. Proverbs 4:23 (NKJV) says "Keep your heart with all diligence for out of it spring the issues of life." What you let into your heart determines the condition of your life. No matter where you are in your relationship with God, guarding your heart is imperative to developing intimacy with God.

Out of our hearts springs the issues of life. The things that come from our hearts reveal who we really are and what's inside of us. That means what is going on in your life, good or bad, is determined by what you let in your heart. There are many ways we can let things into our hearts. Some of them include what we hear and see. Therefore, guarding our heart can consist of monitoring what we watch, and what we listen to.

I want you to think about your life right now. Are you happy with where you are? If not, can you think of some choices you have made that caused you to be where you are? For example, I was tormented by negative emotions in an unhealthy relationship. I was depressed and filled with anxiety. When I evaluated my life, I found that my unhappiness was mainly caused by remaining in the relationship. Choosing to stay in a relationship that was draining and unsatisfying led to more problems than it was worth.

Once I made the decision to get closer to God and remove myself from the relationship, my life improved. If you are happy with your life, can you point to decisions you made that improved your quality of life? In the example I just gave, I made a choice to separate myself from a negative situation and it had lasting benefits. Decisions are powerful and we make decisions daily that either improve or hinder our lives and our walk with God.

Guarding your heart is one of the most important ways to develop and maintain intimacy with Jesus. You have the power to keep your heart pure. God is not a soccer goalie blocking all the shots and keeping all of the bad things out of your heart. You are the goalie of your own heart. You get to keep out the things that you don't want in it. We all have to take responsibility for the choices we make in life.

Where you are in life today is a result of the choices you have made. Some people prefer to play the victim and blame others for where they are. I know that sometimes bad things happen in life that we can't control. But we get to choose our attitudes and responses to what happens in life. I am so grateful that God has given us the ability to make our own choices. He is not a puppet-master. He doesn't pull the strings and make all the choices. He gives us a free will to choose how we will respond.

Proverbs 4:20-21 (NKJV) says "My son, give attention to my words; Incline your ear to my sayings. Do not let them depart from your eyes; Keep them in the midst of your heart; for they are life to those who find them, and health to all their flesh." The book of Proverbs is filled with wisdom and instruction for living a good, godly life. In this scripture, we are encouraged to give attention to God's words. We do this by reading the Bible.

Reading the word of God keeps us close to Him and transforms us. It makes our lives better because we become more like Him. God's words are life. In John 6:63 (NKJV) Jesus says the words that He speaks are spirit and life. When we read the Bible, we are putting life into our hearts. We have to be sure that we are being diligent to read the word of God and not letting it depart from our eyes.

I know that many people struggle with reading the Bible. It can be hard to understand and because of a lack of understanding, some find it boring. If you struggle with reading the Bible, one of the steps you can take to combat this issue would be to ask the Holy Spirit for revelation. John 14:26 (NKJV) says that the Holy Spirit will teach you all things and bring to your remembrance all the things Jesus has said to us. The Holy Spirit is our helper and He helps us to live according to God's ways. You can also pray like David that God would open your eyes to see the wonderful truths in His word. (Psalm 119:18 NLT).

In the first few years of my Christian life, I struggled with enjoying reading the Bible. Although I read it, it didn't come alive in my life. It was hard to remember and I often fell asleep while reading it. Things began to change when I decided to take a break from social media and deactivate all my social media accounts. During that time, I tried to read the Bible daily and as much as possible. Every time I felt the urge to get on social media, I would read a scripture on the Bible App.

In the weeks before I decided to take a social media break, every time I got on Facebook or Instagram I would feel uncomfortable. Usually, when God is bringing conviction to my heart, I simply feel that I shouldn't be doing something. An alarm doesn't go off nor do I hear a loud voice from the sky, I just feel uncomfortable. So, I decided that I would decrease my social media time and increase the amount of time that I spent reading the word of God. I was in a place in my relationship with God where I really wanted to get closer to Him, so I eventually deactivated my accounts.

After a few weeks, I reactivated my social media accounts and they felt foreign to me. God then revealed to me how much social media impacted my relationship with Him and my self-image. I looked at other people and compared myself to them. I was jealous and chasing after superficial things. A few weeks later I decided to give up social media completely. It was difficult at first, but as time went on it became easier. It didn't matter that I didn't know the latest trend on Instagram or that people didn't understand my decision. My life was being changed and I was closer to God than ever before.

If you have used social media, it's more than likely you have experienced some negative situation that arose as a result of something you saw. Maybe you saw something that someone wrote or a picture that was posted that caused an argument. Maybe you saw nearly naked pictures that caused you to lust after someone. I had a friend that would constantly post perverted photos. On a number of occasions, I would come out of church and look at my phone and the image would be stuck in my head.

I finally decided enough was enough. I valued my relationship with God more than I valued getting likes on a photo or knowing what people were posting in their stories. When I deleted my accounts, I was showing God that I didn't want those images to cling to me. I was saying with my actions that I no longer wanted to associate with wickedness. What He had to say to me was far better than anything anyone could ever post.

Radical change requires boldness. Intimacy with God requires boldness. I absolutely love what King David said in Psalm 101:3-4 (NKJV) "I will set nothing wicked before my eyes; I hate the work of those who fall away; It shall not cling to me. A perverse heart shall depart from me; I will not know wickedness." This is a great example of what it looks like to guard your heart. To keep it from the things that would corrupt it or turn it away from God.

Once I made the decision in my heart to step away from social media, the Bible came alive. I remembered scriptures so much easier and God really began to speak to me through the Word. God's voice became clearer and easier to understand. I began to see myself the way He designed me. I had more encounters with God and my appetite for His presence increased.

I don't want you to think that you have to give up social media to have a close relationship with God. I needed to take a break from social media for that season. I now have active accounts but when I feel led, I take breaks or restrict my usage. I hope my testimony encourages you to guard your heart more carefully and be mindful of what you are doing in your life that could be hindering your relationship with God.

There were also TV shows that I enjoyed that I gave up to be closer to God. I no longer watched tv shows with graphic sex scenes or tons of violence. I stopped looking at and giving my attention to things that did not bring me closer to God. You may not feel the need to take these steps but this is what it took for me to get closer to God. The scripture I referred to in Proverbs 4:20 says "give attention to my words". What are you giving your attention to?

In Proverbs 4:20 (NKJV) it also says "incline your ear to my sayings". What are you listening to? Many Christians listen to ungodly or secular music without realizing the impact it has on their spirits. That is music by people who live in the world and have no religion. 1 John 2:16 (NKJV) says "For all that is in the world-the lust of the flesh, the lust of the eyes, and the pride of life-is not of the Father but is of the world." Does the music you listen to make you want to have sex after you listen to it? Does it make you envious and desire to be wealthy? Does it make you feel like your life is your own and you can do whatever you want without consequence?

Along with that, who are you listening to? Do the people you spend the most time with serve God too? Are they inspiring you to go after the things of God or live life based on what feels or seems good? Do they put you down or build you up? Do they encourage you to dishonor God? This could also refer to the podcasts or influencers and celebrities that you listen to. The voices you choose to listen to will shape your life.

We have an enemy, the devil, who works through deception. He wants you to think that the things you watch and listen to won't hurt you, but that is far from the truth. Ephesians 6:12 says "For we do not wrestle against flesh and blood, but against principalities, against powers, against the rulers of the darkness of this age, against spiritual hosts of wickedness in the heavenly places." The things that are fighting against us can't always be seen by us.

I believe many Christians struggle because not enough of us are truly allowing Jesus to be Lord over every area of our lives. Sometimes we restrict His lordship in our own lives. For example, it is acceptable to glorify God for two hours every Sunday or maybe even for an additional two hours during a home group or Bible study, but what about everything else we do? I have found this time of singleness to be a blessing because I have been able to make Jesus the Lord of every area of my life. Is it always easy? Definitely not, but it is worth the cost.

There are three important areas that are central to guarding the heart: finances, entertainment and relationships. They typically make Christians uncomfortable because they reflect who we really serve. Let's look at them.

Finances

I want you to take a moment and answer these questions honestly:

- Do you always tithe (give the first 10%) from all of the increase you receive from God?
- Do you give regularly to ministries or people in need?
- Do you always invite God into your finances and ask Him for wisdom?

If you can't answer yes to these questions, then this is an area that you may need to develop in. When you are single, it is the perfect time to work on your finances. I know some people who believe that their financial stability will come when they are married. But marriage is not the answer to financial issues. In fact, financial issues are usually the cause of many marital issues. This time is a great opportunity to learn how to grow and manage money with God.

You can also work to be a giver and grow in generosity during this time. Tithe to your church consistently, give to nonprofits and help out people in need. Sponsor a child, buy meals for the homeless or whatever else God may put on your heart. Ask God where He wants you to invest your resources and go on a journey with Him to make an impact with your money. Don't just spend all your money on what you think you should, ask God what He wants you to do with the money He has given you.

If you are in debt this is also the time to work on paying it off. Get your credit straight. Ask God for wisdom for your finances. James 1:5 (NKJV) says "If any of you lack wisdom, let him ask of God who gives to all liberally and without reproach, and it will be given to him." If you have negative spending habits, begin to work it out now. Live in the present and focus on your financial stability. And most of all, make God the Lord or Master over this area of your life.

Jesus spoke about money often in the Bible. He used the topic of money as a way of demonstrating the heart of God and the heart of man. Money alone isn't good or bad. It's how we use it that determines the outcome. What we do with our money matters to God and it is an indicator of our relationship with God.

Entertainment

Everyone has different convictions and standards for how they live life. Like finances, making Jesus the Lord over how you are entertained is a personal matter. For example, I know some Christians who watch horror films. I do not. My rule of thumb is to stop if I don't have peace about something and to proceed if I do. As I share my thoughts on entertainment, I believe that the Holy Spirit will speak to you about how He wants you to manage this part of your life.

Take a moment and answer these questions honestly.

- How much time do you spend on social media?
- Would you feel comfortable watching your favorite shows or movies with Jesus?
- Does the music you listen to glorify God?

How we are entertained is crucial to our success as Christians. It is also connected to how intimate we are with our Heavenly Father. Mark 4 discusses the Parable of the Sower and the different grounds that a seed can be sown on. Mark 4:18 (NKJV) says "Now these are the ones sown among thorns; they are the ones who hear the word, and the cares of this world, the deceitfulness of riches and the desires for other things entering in choke the word, and it becomes unfruitful."

Essentially Jesus is saying that we can hear God's Word but get distracted and enticed by things of the world and suddenly the things of God are less important or desirable. If you want true intimacy with Christ, choose to be entertained by the things that God approves of and not the things of this world. Listen to worship music, watch family-oriented TV shows, limit your social media time and increase your Word time. There are many things you can do that are fun and entertaining that don't grieve the Holy Spirit. Ask Him to show you if anything you are being entertained by needs to be renounced. Then ask Him to guide you to things that are pleasing to Him and entertaining to you.

Relationships

Take some time to evaluate your relationships by answering these questions:

- Do you have mentors or people who are pouring into you and helping you develop your relationship with Christ?
- Do you have godly friendships with other Christians?
- Do you spend more time around people in the body of Christ than people in the world?
- Are you involved in any relationships that God is telling you to break free from?

This area is important to cover because our relationships have great influence over who we become. If you truly want to be close to God, you should surround yourself with people who desire the same. Proverbs 13:20 (NKJV) says "He who walks with wise men will be wise, but the companion of fools will be destroyed." Psalm 1:1 (NKJV) states "Blessed is the man who walks not in the counsel of the ungodly, nor stands in the path of sinners, nor sits in the seat of the scornful."

I speak to you from experience because I have given up many important relationships to be closer to God. The closer I got to Him, I realized that some of my friendships would have to end. It was painful to end these relationships but God blessed me more than I thought possible. I now have many Christian friends and mentors who pour into my life. I also have friends who are unbelievers that have been blessings to my life. Everyone who is in my life now has been put there by God because I let Him be Lord. I let Him decide who should and shouldn't be in my life. I encourage you to take the time to evaluate your relationships with God and eliminate any unhealthy relationships from your life, romantic or platonic.

As a woman in my 30s, I have seen people rush into romantic relationships because they are desperate to get married and have children. As a result, they miss the perfect will of God. God gives us a free will to make our own decisions, but what we decide proves whether or not He is the Lord over our lives. In the season of singleness, it is so easy to rationalize relationships that we know deep in our hearts are not pleasing to God. If you are in a relationship with someone you know you shouldn't be, then I urge you to let it go.

I once had a very close friendship that I felt God leading me to separate from. The closer I got to God the more I realized how toxic our relationship was. My eyes were opened and I started to feel uncomfortable being around them. However, it was very difficult for me to let this relationship go. I didn't want to offend them, I was afraid of confrontation and I was really concerned about what they would think of me. But I got to the point where I wanted God more than the relationship. As I cut those ties God began to bring people into my life that encouraged me to go after the things of God.

This is also a great time to make sure you have mentors and spiritual leaders that can pour into you. I would not be where I am today without the leaders God placed in my life. Early in my journey with the Lord, I realized I needed accountability and people who were further ahead than me to help me get to where I wanted to be. There have been times where God instructed me to ask particular people to mentor me. Even though it felt awkward, I let Him be Lord and chose to obey. If you don't have a mentor or spiritual leader then ask God to highlight someone to you. Pray that God will bring you someone that will help you get closer to Him.

In the time of singleness, it is crucial that you make choices that will set you up for success. If the people you hang out with grieve the Holy Spirit inside of you, then it's time to evaluate your friendships. Show Jesus that He is what matters most to you. The Bible says in Matthew 10:37-39 (NKJV), "He who loves father or mother more than Me is not worthy of Me. And he who loves son or daughter more than Me is not worthy of Me. And he who does not take his cross and follow after Me is not worthy of Me. He who finds his life will lose it, and he who loses his life for My sake will find it." This scripture says it all. If you value any relationship in your life more than your relationship with God then you are not worthy of Him. When you lose friendships and relationships to become closer to God, He will bless you.

Overall, guarding your heart is an ongoing process. It is not somewhere we arrive. Seasons change and what is necessary in one season may not be in another. No matter what, it is important to listen to God and be led by peace.

Think about it…

- How well have you been guarding your heart?
- How will making Him the Lord over all areas of your life bring you closer to Him?
- What lifestyle change can you make to guard your heart more carefully?

Prayer

Father, I thank you for giving me a free will and the ability to make my own choices. I pray that with this freedom, I will live responsibly and make choices that bring me closer to you. Help me to see and think clearly. Help me to use discretion in the area of my finances, how I'm entertained and in my relationships. I submit these areas to you and I pray for a greater amount of wisdom. I want to live a life that is pleasing to you. I pray that you would show me any area where I need to pivot and give me grace to make the change.

Chapter 6

Clean House

When you intentionally give up an area for Jesus
to clean, He will make it more beautiful
than you could imagine.

The time of singleness is an opportune time to clear out the clutter from every area of your life. Think of your heart as a house. Jesus stands at the door and knocks, and you let Him in when you accept Him as Lord. But do you ever let Him past the living room? Have you allowed Him into every room, every part of your heart? This chapter will discuss how necessary it is that God has full access to your life so that He can clear out anything that is a hindrance to your relationship with Him.

One of the main reasons that people don't allow Jesus into every area of their lives is because we want to clean up for Him even though He is the one who actually does the cleaning. We desire to have it all together before we present ourselves to Him. However, we hinder purity and wholeness when we don't let Jesus into the secret places of our hearts. Psalm 139:23-24 (NKJV) declares "Search me, O God, and know my heart; Try me and know my anxieties; and see if there is any wicked way in me, and lead me in the way everlasting." This is the attitude we must develop. Search me God, know me God, show me what needs to change and help me to change it.

Jesus desires for us to be pure and clean in every area of our lives. He knows how messy our lives are, and what He needs to do to clean us up. The good news is that He doesn't leave us to figure anything out on our own. We just have to make sure that we are willing to let Him go to those places. Don't stop Him from going deeper because you are hiding something. He wants to continue moving through each room in the home of your heart so that you are "perfect and complete and lacking nothing." (James 1:4 NKJV)

To clear out the clutter in your spiritual life you can start by eliminating clutter in your natural life. You may begin with the clutter in your home. No matter how large or small of a place you live in, take the time to remove the junk that is taking up space. Donate old clothes you no longer wear or have a garage sale. You could even put some items up for sale online. Go through piles of mail, clean out your cabinets and refrigerator. Clean out all of your closets and your car. Do whatever you need to do to make sure the spaces you spend time in are free from clutter.

We can clear the clutter from our souls and spirits by spending time with God. Isaiah 61:3 (NKJV) says He will give us "beauty for ashes, the oil of joy for mourning, the garment of praise for the spirit of heaviness." That means we can take all the junk and the clutter from our lives, give it to Jesus and He will exchange it for something wonderful. The more time we spend with Him, the more we become like Him. When you intentionally give up an area for Jesus to clean, He will make it more beautiful than you could ever imagine.

Maybe you've tracked some dirt in from your past and now you have a big stain on your carpet. Let Him take care of that for you. Perhaps you've put up some extra walls from past disappointments that make it hard for Him to move in every room. Let Jesus be your carpenter and take down those walls and open up the space. God is for you no matter what, and nothing can separate you from the love of God. He is not afraid of our messy, ugly, dark, smelly sin. You will find that once the clutter leaves your life you will hear from God more easily.

Sometime ago God gave me a vision of the Holy Spirit moving into a house. The house was my heart. It was dark inside and it had really ugly furniture. It was unappealing and not a place where I would expect anyone to want to stay a while. Although it looked bad on the inside, He was moving in some beautiful pieces of furniture. In order to fit the new items inside, He said the old, ugly items had to be removed. I looked around the room and even though I was happy to receive the new furniture, I didn't want to give up my old junk. How many times does this happen in our lives? God is trying to remove something that is outdated and no longer serves us from our hearts but we hold onto it.

I can speak from experience and say one of the things that I didn't want to give up was my relationship with my ex-boyfriend. I wanted to hold on even though I knew it was time to let it go. God was clear with me that He had something better but I was resisting. Why did I resist? For the same reason that people all over the world go back to people that they know they shouldn't be with. Soul ties.

Soul Ties

One of the major ways the enemy traps people is through soul ties. A soul tie is the bonding of your soul to another soul. Soul ties come as a result of a close emotional or sexual relationship. God intended for soul ties to bring a husband and wife closer together. Genesis 2:24 (NKJV) says "That is why a man leaves his father and mother and is united to his wife, and they become one flesh." They become one flesh as a result of being united. This is an example of a healthy, godly, soul tie.

When you spend a lot of time with a person you form a connection with them. You start to think and talk and act like that person. If you have sex, that connection will increase to new levels. That person may consume your thoughts and you may want to be around them all the time. These feelings were intended for a husband and wife but unfortunately many people have soul ties with people that are not their intended husband or wife.

Any time you have sex with someone, you form a soul tie with them. That's why you know when they are going to call or you think about them before they show up. Your souls are joined together. Your soul is your mind, your will and your emotions. Once your soul is joined with another, they have access to your mind (your thoughts), your will (your decisions and choices) and your emotions (how you act/feel).

I was in a relationship with a guy from the ages of 14-20. It lasted through high school and most of my college years. As a result of spending so much time with this person and because we were intimate, my soul was tied to him. It took a while for me to break free from the soul tie, mainly because I had no idea what a soul tie was. I just thought that we had a special bond and used it as evidence for why we should be together.

Once I became a Christian, God helped me to see that I needed to be free from the soul tie. I have spent lots of time in prayer forgiving him, myself and receiving God's forgiveness. I have broken all ties to him and spent time renouncing every covenant and agreement that I made regarding a relationship with Him. And through the power of God I am free!

If you have ungodly soul ties to people from your past, then God desires to set you free. He wants to clear out the clutter of ungodly soul ties. This may not be the first time you have learned about soul ties but there still might be a deeper level of freedom that God wants you to experience.

Jesus came to set the captives free. Although this is commonly quoted by Christians all over the world, not many people walk in the fullness of this truth. When the bible refers to captives, it's not only referring to people who are slaves or in a physical jail. It means people who are in any form of bondage.

Bondage is a result of sin and all of our life experiences that do not align with God's will. Bondage can come from many sources like things that have happened in our past when we were children, or bad decisions in our teenage years. There are countless ways that the enemy traps people and causes clutter in our lives but ultimately Jesus came so that we would be free from it all.

Ephesians 4:27 (AMP) states "Leave no [such] room *or* foothold for the devil [give no opportunity to him]." This scripture applies to every area of our lives. The enemy wants to keep us bound to sin and to destroy our lives. He actively looks for ways to enter our lives so that he can have his way. This scripture is telling us not to give him an opportunity. Once you sever your ungodly soul tie, the enemy has no entryway through that person. He can no longer use them to torment you and lead you away from the will of God.

Unhealthy soul ties cause clutter to our souls. They hinder our ability to hear from God. They also hinder our ability to be intimate with Him. One way to begin to get free from the clutter of an unhealthy soul tie is to cut off contact with the person. It may be difficult at first but it is necessary for where God wants to take you. When I was breaking away from the soul tie, I decreased the time that I spent on the phone with him, and the face-to-face contact.

Instead of talking with him every night, I used my time to seek God's help to break free. As I spent time with God consistently, my desires began to change. It was no longer a fight to talk to God instead of him. 2 Corinthians 3:17 (NKJV) says "Now the Lord is the Spirit and where the Spirit of the

Lord is there is liberty." As I worshiped God and read the word and spent time with Him, He liberated me.

The time of singleness is the time to break free from soul ties. It is the perfect opportunity to let God move in and clean us up. If you are reading this book, then you clearly desire to be closer to God. You want your life to change. The good news is that if you are struggling with a bad relationship or sexual bondage, you can be free. Here is a sample prayer you can pray to begin to break the ungodly soul ties in your life:

> Father I come to you in the name of Jesus believing that you can and will set me free from all ungodly soul ties. I repent of all emotional and sexual sin I have committed. I pray that you will forgive me for being outside of your will and entering into an ungodly soul tie. I choose to forgive every person that I have had an ungodly relationship with. Father, thank you for your forgiveness and I receive it in Jesus' name.

Another important aspect of cleaning house is conquering sexual sin. Unfortunately, we live in a culture/generation that is overly sexual. Like me, you may have given yourself over to the temptation of sex before marriage. Before I gave my life to Christ I didn't value holiness and purity. I had no desire to please God let alone offer my body as a sacrifice to Him. I have compassion for women who have had to break free from sexual sin because of my journey.

When I fully decided to go after Christ, I was told that I would go through a process of sanctification. I was told that

God would remove things from my heart that were not like Him and replace it with what would please Him. I was excited about being renewed and purifying myself. The only problem was that I couldn't find the tools I needed to overcome the sin. I felt that I was missing out on the strategies and proven methods that could help me conquer my battle with lust and perversion. Besides being told not to do it because it was bad, I didn't know what to do. I didn't feel like I had what I needed to win. I stumbled through, finding scriptures and praying to God for help. Every once in a while, when the urges became overwhelming, or if I was having recurring sexual dreams, then I would reach out to a leader. But I struggled and often felt guilty and condemned.

I want to be open about my journey and provide women with strategies to claim victory in this area. You may not have struggled or been tempted in this area and that's okay. But many Christians are fighting silent battles and just need more ammunition. As I have mentored and led people over the years, I have noticed that many feel too afraid or ashamed to ask for help.

So, here's the deal. I haven't had sex in over twelve years. Although much time has passed, my urges and desires have remained. Some days are harder than others but I have come a long way and learned to manage my sex drive. I have not masturbated or watched porn since committing my life to Christ. One of the driving factors for abstaining from sex and maintaining sexual purity all these years has been my intimacy with God. Because I know and love Him, I want to do what pleases him.

At times, my fear of God's punishment and rejection has motivated me to stay pure. I was scared to disappoint Him and terrified of what my leaders and peers would think of me if I engaged in sexual sin. But at this point in my walk with God, I'm compelled more by my devotion to the Lord than my aversion for punishment and judgment. Loving God with all of my heart, soul and mind induces holiness in me. I pray that you also will remain pure because of your intimacy with God.

Through trial and error, I learned what works for me. I learned more about my emotional and physical needs and how to get them met in a healthy, God pleasing way. I learned my triggers and ways to avoid them. For example, I avoid certain types of music and don't watch sex scenes in movies because I know it will make me start thinking about sex. Fighting against sexual sin is an ongoing battle and we all must find the right weapons to help us succeed.

If you are struggling to overcome sexual sin, I pray that you find this information useful. The Holy Spirit can and will teach you anything you need to know. He will help you to conquer whatever you may be facing. If you feel like you need more help or greater accountability, please reach out to someone you trust in your community.

In moments where I am feeling weak and battling sexual thoughts and urges, the first thing I normally do is check in with my body because I am human. I have hormones and emotions and a sex drive. God created me with these things for a purpose. I think to myself, am I ovulating? Are my hormones causing this in any way? God designed women's bodies to reproduce and our hormones play a role in that process. Sometimes, my body is just functioning correctly and doing its job to help me make a baby.

If it's not hormonal, I then think, what is it that my body wants or what emotional needs do I have that are not being met?

Sometimes, my body wants to experience pleasure. Sometimes, I crave intimacy and connection and want to be desired. These occurrences increase when I spend less time with the Lord. And at times, in order to get my needs met, my mind starts to fantasize past sexual encounters.

When I let my imagination run wild, I can become aroused and gain pleasure from remembering a sexual experience. In those moments I always have a choice. Although I may have a strong desire to continue meditating on that sexual encounter, I will literally feel a pull to stop. 1 Corinthians 10:13 (NKJV) states "No temptation has overtaken you except such as is common to man; but God is faithful, who will not allow you to be tempted beyond what you are able, but with the temptation will also make the way of escape, that you may be able to bear it."

Every time I choose to open my ears to the Lord's voice, He gives me a way out. The only time I fall victim is when I don't fight back and take my thoughts captive. When I don't try I lose. When I try, I always overcome. James 4:7 says "Therefore submit to God. Resist the devil and he will flee from you." During that time, I often ask the Holy Spirit to help me and fill every place in my soul and body that is lacking.

If you want to please God and live according to His will for your life then you must live pure. These scriptures from 2 Timothy 2:20-21(Amplified Bible, Classic Edition) say it all, "But in a great house there are not only vessels of gold and silver, but also [utensils] of wood and earthenware, and some for honorable *and* noble [use] and some for menial *and* ignoble [use]. So, whoever cleanses himself [from what is ignoble *and* unclean, who separates himself from contact with contaminating and corrupting influences] will [then himself] be a vessel set apart *and* useful for honorable *and* noble purposes, consecrated *and* profitable to the Master, fit *and* ready for any good work." Cleaning up sexual sin requires honesty and vulnerability. It can be very messy, hard and embarrassing. But it is necessary and is part of the formation of an intimate relationship with God. I tell Him when I am struggling with lust. I tell Him when I don't feel like waiting anymore. I'm open about my desire to turn away from His will when I get tired of resisting my natural urges. In Psalm 32:5 (NIV) David wrote "Then I acknowledged my sin to you and did not cover up my iniquity. I said, "I will confess my transgressions to the LORD." And you forgave the guilt of my sin." I don't sweep anything under the rug or try to downplay my actions. I admit my sin and ask for forgiveness.

I don't keep secrets from God. I tell Him everything and don't hide anything. There is no point in even trying to hold anything back because He sees and knows all. Hebrews 4:13 (NLT) states "Nothing in all creation is hidden from God. Everything is naked and exposed before his eyes, and He is the one to whom we are accountable." Attempting to shield sin is pointless because we will have to answer to God about it.

Another important part of my process has been exposing my battles and allowing others to speak into my life. By being vulnerable and letting my friends and mentors know what I am going through, it has held me accountable and helped me to not feel isolated. When I let people in, I can ask for prayer and encouragement instead of trying to be strong and face it on my own. Proverbs 28:13 (NLT) reads "People who conceal their sins will not prosper, but if they confess and turn from them, they will receive mercy."

Meditating on scripture has been an additional key to my success, especially when dealing with fantasies and urges. In the moments where my mind starts wandering to things it shouldn't, I speak the word out loud. I read these scriptures as many times as I need to and say them out loud.

Here are some scriptures that I use to fight sexual sin:

> Psalm 51:10 (NKJV) "Create in me a clean heart, O God, And renew a steadfast spirit within me."

> 1 Thessalonians 4:3-4 (AMP) "For this is the will of God, that you be sanctified [separated and set apart from sin]: that you abstain *and* back away from sexual immorality; that each of you know how to control his own body in holiness and honor [being available for God's purpose and separated from things profane]."

> 1 Thessalonians 4:7 (AMP) "For God has not called us to impurity, but to holiness [to be dedicated, and set apart by behavior that pleases Him, whether in public or in private]".

> Romans 12:1 (NLT) "And so, dear brothers and sisters, I plead with you to give your bodies to God because of all he has done for you. Let them be a living and holy sacrifice—the kind he will find acceptable. This is truly the way to worship him."

1 Peter 1:15-16 (NKJV) "but as He who called you is holy, you also be holy in all your conduct, because it is written, "Be holy, for I am holy.""

Romans 6:12-13 (NLT) "Do not let sin control the way you live; do not give in to sinful desires. Do not let any part of your body become an instrument of evil to serve sin. Instead, give yourselves completely to God, for you were dead, but now you have new life. So use your whole body as an instrument to do what is right for the glory of God."

1 Corinthians 6:18-20 (NLT) "Run from sexual sin! No other sin so clearly affects the body as this one does. For sexual immorality is a sin against your own body. Don't you realize that your body is the temple of the Holy Spirit, who lives in you and was given to you by God? You do not belong to yourself, for God bought you with a high price. So you must honor God with your body."

Philippians 4:8 (NIV) "Finally, brothers and sisters, whatever is true, whatever is noble, whatever is right, whatever is pure, whatever is lovely, whatever is admirable—if anything is excellent or praiseworthy—think about such things."

Abstaining from sex the past 12 years has been no easy feat. I am doing a hard thing. As I've dated, I've encountered men that have pushed my boundaries and desired to commit sexual sin. One guy in particular, would send me pictures with his shirt off and inappropriate texts. It usually happened if we were talking late at night. I was always very firm with him about my boundaries but it began to get harder to resist him. I wish that I would have closed the door on him sooner.

While we didn't have sex, I compromised and fell short of my standard and God's. Jesus told the crowd during one of His teachings "You have heard the commandment that says, 'You must not commit adultery.' But I say, anyone who even looks at a woman with lust has already committed adultery with her in his heart." Matthew 5:27-28 (NLT) This verse is sobering and should make us all see how serious God is about sexual sin.

God's version of purity isn't just refraining from having sex. It's all encompassing and gets down to our thoughts and motives. His version of purity addresses what's in our hearts, what we desire. He doesn't just desire for us to not have sex. He wants us to steer clear of lust and not let it corrupt us from the inside. Purity isn't only reflected in our outward actions, it's what's inside of us. It's reflected in what we think about. God can see every part of us, nothing is hidden from Him.

As I continued to date this man, I struggled to fight off fantasies and the onslaught of sexual thoughts that would inundate me. When we were together, he couldn't keep his hands off of me. I refused to kiss him because I knew it would only lead to more. I made sure that we were never in a house alone because I honestly didn't think I could resist the temptation. One day he even admitted that he would try to have sex with me if we were ever home alone.

I fought back with prayer, worship and the word. I told my friends about my struggle and tried my best to stay in the light. They reminded me of who I am and who God called me to be. My desire to please God and fulfill my purpose helped me to stay focused. My housemates and I also agreed not to have men at the house past midnight. Additionally, we set a rule of no cuddling on the couch and no going to bedrooms with the door closed. We set the boundaries ahead of time to protect our purity.

Ultimately, I had to end the relationship. It was too much for me and I knew that a true man of God would not cause me to sin in that way. I tolerated him longer than I should have because I was lonely, he was attractive and I genuinely enjoyed his company. I was tested and weak. But I depended on the Lord and He preserved me. Jude 1:24 (NLT) says "Now all glory to God, who is able to keep you from falling away and will bring you with great joy into his glorious presence without a single fault." God is faithful to help us overcome.

In summary, I have abstained from sex and dealt with my sexual urges by being open with God and confessing my struggles to Him. Also, by being motivated to pursue holiness because of my love for Him. I let others into my process and allow them to pray and encourage me. As well as taking my thoughts captive and meditating on scripture.

God desires for you to be free and uncontaminated from this world. He doesn't want us full of clutter or bound to any sin. I pray that God would give you a revelation of any area in your life that He wants to clean. I pray that you would be open to the cleansing process and that you would walk in greater levels of purity, holiness and intimacy as a result. Matthew 5:8 (NIV) says "Blessed are the pure in heart, for they will see God." May your clean heart allow you to see God more clearly.

<h1 style="text-align:center">Think about it…</h1>

- What is the one area of your life that needs to be cleaned the most?
- Is there anything you are doing that is hindering God from moving all the way in?
- Are you free from all ungodly soul ties? If not, what steps should you take to get free?

Prayer

God, I desire to be pure and holy just like you. Please help me to clear out any sin and clutter in my soul. I will be intentional about letting you have access to every part of my life. I won't hold anything back from you. God, I pray that you would help me to fight against sexual sin by giving me the right tools. Please help me to yield to your voice when I am being tempted. Please show me who I can be accountable to and who I should partner with on this journey. Help me to be set apart and overcome every battle I face against my purity.

Chapter 7

Develop Your Self-Image

Love yourself, all of yourself.

Learning to see yourself the way God does is an important journey to take while you are single. Loving who God created you to be is key to a healthy relationship with Him, yourself and others. Matthew 22:37-39 (NLT) reads "You must love the Lord your God with all your heart, all your soul, and all your mind. This is the first and greatest commandment. A second is equally important: Love your neighbor as yourself." If you don't love yourself well, how can you love God and others well?

While you are single, I encourage you to develop a healthy self-image and discover more of who you are in Christ. As a single woman, you have the opportunity to spend considerable amounts of time with the Lord. Your time with God will transform you and allow you to see Him and yourself better. He will help you to see the ways in which you can impact the lives of others and show them who He is.

Healthy relationships consist of individuals who are not only secure with themselves, they also like who they are. If you don't like who you are, it will surely manifest within your relationship with God because you behave according to what you believe. If you believe you are right with God and loved by Him, you will behave that way. But if you believe you are unloved and unworthy, your actions will demonstrate this. You will shy away from His presence and speak negatively about yourself. But once you view yourself the way God views you, you can be secure and operate in confidence.

When you are secure and confident in who you are, you don't work hard to be accepted. You know that you are loved and chosen and this shapes how you operate with God, how you view yourself and how you relate to others. Having a healthy self-image is rooted in knowing your identity. When you know who you are and what God says about you, it anchors you.

In Numbers 13, Moses sent spies to check out the promised land that God had given them. When the spies returned, the majority of them doubted their ability to possess the land because there were giants and other obstacles. But Caleb, one of the spies, had a healthy self-image. He believed he could accomplish the task. In Numbers 13:30 (NKJV) he said "Let us go up at once and take possession, for we are well able to overcome it."

However, the rest of the spies said "There we saw the giants...and we were like grasshoppers in our own sight, and so we were in their sight." Their view of themselves hindered their ability to possess what God had given them! Do you view yourself as a grasshopper even though God believes you are well able to overcome giants? In what areas of your life is your view of yourself different from God's?

Our original design is laid out for us in Genesis. Genesis 1:26-27 (NKJV) reads "Then God said, "Let Us make man in Our image, according to Our likeness; let them have dominion over the fish of the sea, over the birds of the air, and over the cattle, over all the earth and over every creeping thing that creeps on the earth." So God created man in His own image; in the image of God He created him; male and female He created them." We were formed with purpose and intention. God's aim was that we would be like Him.

Being created in God's likeness, in His image, is the foundation of our existence. Knowing this truth is what establishes everything we believe about ourselves. This is what shapes our identity, and is the lens through which we must view ourselves. We are image-bearers, we carry God's likeness. Our self-worth relies upon this knowledge.

How ridiculous would it be if a millionaire was homeless? Imagine if a person had the ability and the finances to live a much better life but instead they believed that they were poor and stayed on the street. It seems absurd, but that's what happens to many people who don't have a correct self-image. If you don't see yourself the way God sees you, then your ability to fulfill your potential will be hindered.

God wants you to see yourself the way He designed you. He wants you to know all the good things He has created you for. In my experience, as I got closer to God, I began to see myself more accurately. The more time I spent learning the truth about who He is, the clearer my identity came into focus. Having a healthy self-image will allow you to come into alignment with your destiny.

One major event that helped me develop a healthy self-image, happened during a women's conference at my church. We completed an activity where we wrote down what God said about us. Instrumental worship music played as we prayed that God would speak to us. Then we got quiet and wrote down what we heard God speaking. I wasn't sure that I was really hearing from God, but I just wrote down what I heard anyway. Sometimes I heard a word in a whisper, other times I saw a picture in my mind of that word.

The words I wrote down were: faithfulness, righteousness, joy, peace, perseverance, abundance, favor, love, patience and power. Once I saw them on paper, I had a choice to believe it was from God or not. God is good and whatever He says about me is good so I chose to believe. Sometime later, God led me to use those words to write declarations on sticky notes and put them on the mirror in my bedroom. When I needed to be reminded of what God said about me, I looked at my mirror and read one of the declarations. It is important that you value what God says about you and you remind yourself of it daily.

I encourage you to take some time to hear from God as well. Carve out a time where you can be alone and uninterrupted. You can play music or just sit quietly. Let Him speak to you. Depending on where you are in your walk with Him, this may be challenging at first. But, don't let fear and doubt block you from receiving what God has for you. Whatever He says, write it down. Remember that God is kind and patient and He loves you.

After your time with Him, I also want to encourage you to put those words on sticky notes and post them around your home. Put them on the mirror you use to get dressed in the morning. Look at yourself in the mirror and say what God says about you. I promise it will change your life.

I want to share a story that further emphasizes the importance of reminding yourself of who God says you are. The sticky notes I wrote were on my mirror for months. I looked at them every day and reminded myself of the words God had spoken to me. One weekend, a few of my family members were coming over and I decided to take the notes down. I didn't feel like explaining what they meant and I felt it was very personal. So, down they went behind my jewelry box. The days turned to weeks and the sticky notes began to collect dust.

In time, I began to struggle in areas that I previously had victory over. For example, I had no joy or peace and I was noticeably impatient. I didn't feel powerful or loved by God. Once I grew tired of the struggle, I asked the Lord for clarity. The Holy Spirit then reminded me that I needed to put the sticky notes back up. I wasn't viewing myself in light of what God said and had forgotten who I was.

Then God led me to James 1:23-24 (NKJV) where it says "For if anyone is a hearer of the word and not a doer, he is like a man observing his natural face in a mirror; for he observes himself, goes away, and immediately forgets what kind of man he was." So, I plucked them from behind my jewelry box, blew off the dust and put them back in their original position. The next time my family came to visit, I explained their meaning and one of them liked it so much that she has sticky notes on her mirror too!

I would also like to encourage you to write down a list of declarations to speak over yourself every day. There are many declarations that are readily available on the internet and in books. However, I would like you to assess your own life. Really think about where you are now and where you want to be in the future. What things do you need to cultivate in your life? Maybe you would like to be more disciplined or more patient. Write it down and speak out loud what you want to happen. Here are some examples:

- I delight myself in the word and I meditate on its day and night. I am like a tree planted by the rivers of water. I bring forth fruit in season. My leaf will not wither and whatever I do prospers (Psalm 1:2-3 NKJV)
- The Lord daily loads me with benefits (Psalm 68:19 NKJV)
- The Lord is my Shepherd and I shall not want (Psalm 23:1 NKJV)
- I will do all things without grumbling, faultfinding and complaining (Philippians 2:14 AMPC)
- God did not give me a spirit of timidity but of power and of love and of a calm and well-balanced mind and discipline and self-control (2 Timothy 1:7 AMPC)

Feel free to use these declarations for your own life. The more you see these words and hear these words being spoken out loud, the more you will internalize them. You will agree with these words and believe these words. Your view of yourself will begin to be transformed into the image of God's word.

Another element to developing your self-image is being comfortable in your skin. You should like what you see when you look in the mirror and accept who you are, flaws and all. There was a season where I really struggled with my hair. I had to go through a process to truly love myself and it was difficult. I was constantly straightening my hair, dying it and wearing extensions because I wanted to look a certain way and I didn't want to deal with my natural hair. But God told me "I want you to love yourself, all of yourself, even your hair." I had no clue that I was about to embark on a journey that would transform me from the inside out.

Over the next few months, I began to see how resistant I was to wearing my hair in its natural state. I tried several different hairstyles in an attempt to avoid what I felt I needed to do, which was to cut it all off. Sometime later, I mustered up the courage and got my hair cut. It was the scariest and most liberating thing I have ever done. Each day, I had to look in the mirror and accept who I was and how God made me. I learned to accept and love myself at a deeper level during that season.

I share this story because there may be a journey that God wants to take you on in regards to your self-image. It doesn't have to be physical but it could be. If there is something that you don't like about yourself, seek God about what to do. If there is any area where you feel less than or unworthy, then ask for His help. Use your time as a single person to become as healthy as possible.

I treasure my singleness because I've been able to grow into a more mature and complete version of myself. When I reflect on who I was before Christ, I realize that I didn't know who I was or what God created me for. I didn't see myself as someone who was created after God's likeness and I made choices that reflected my beliefs. I hold myself to a different standard now because I see myself accurately and I operate as an image-bearer. This is what God desires for you as well.

It is important that you have confidence in who God created you to be. It is necessary that you carry yourself in a way that lines up with your beliefs. If you believe you are holy, then act holy. If you believe you are beautiful, take time to care for yourself in a manner that reflects your beliefs. God cares about your self-image and how you view yourself. He wants you to have a correct self-image so that you can impact the world around you.

Think about it...

Here are a few more scriptures about self-image and their translation in declaration form. Use these if necessary but also take the time to make your own list. Read the scriptures or the declarations, over and over until you really start to believe them. When lies come into your head, speak the scriptures out loud. Read them every day for as long as you need to.

Confession #1: I've been created in the image of God

> Genesis 1:27 NKJV "So God created man in
> His own image; in the image of God He created
> them; male and female He created them

Confession #2: I am part of a chosen generation, a royal priesthood, and God's own special people

> 1 Peter 2:9 NKJV "But you are a chosen
> generation, a royal priesthood, a holy nation,
> His own special people, that you may proclaim
> the praises of Him who called you out of
> darkness into His marvelous light

Confession #3: God is mindful of me, He cares for me. I've been crowned with glory and honor

> Psalm 8:4-5 NIV "What is mankind that You
> are mindful of them, human beings that you
> care for them? You have made them a little
> lower than the angels and crowned them with
> glory and honor"

Confession #4: I am a new creation and old things have passed away and all things are new

> 2 Corinthians 5:17 NKJV "Therefore if anyone
> is in Christ, he is a new creation; old things have
> passed away; behold all things have become new."

Confession #5: I am a daughter of God and an heir of God through Christ

Galatians 4:7 NKJV "Therefore you are no longer a slave but a son, and if a son, then an heir of God through Christ"

Prayer

Thank you, God, for creating me in your image and after your likeness. You designed me with intention and you are happy with what you made. I pray that you will help me to love myself fully. You know all of my flaws and the things that I want to improve. I pray that you will help me to overcome self-doubt and grow in confidence. I want to see myself the way that you see me. As I spend more time with you, may I learn the truth about who you have created me to be.

Chapter 8

Pursue the Will of God

You have to trust that what God has for you
is the best option.

I want to start this chapter with some questions for self-reflection. What has God called you to do? What are you pursuing in life? What is it that you desire? What is the focus of your life? How do you make decisions? Do you consult with all of your friends or talk things over with a family member before consulting God? How important is His input in your life choices?

Proverbs 19:21 says "Many are the plans in a person's heart, but it is the LORD's purpose that prevails." (New International Version) We all have desires and plans for how we want things to go in our lives. Sometimes though, what we want doesn't match what God wants for us. In order to grow in intimacy with God and develop a relationship with Him, you have to seek and actively pursue His will for your life.

Being in the will of God requires a deliberate choice. Our choices either lead us toward the will of God or away from His will. Our actions actually prove our love for Him. 1 John 3:18 (NIV) says "Dear children, let us not love with words or speech but with actions and in truth." It is one thing to talk about loving God and doing His will but it is another thing to actually do it. Deuteronomy 30:19 states (NLT) "I call heaven and earth to witness this day against you that I have set before you life and death, the blessings and the curses; therefore choose life, that you and your descendants may live."

God has given us a free will to make our own choices. Our choices lead us to life or they lead us to death. Although He is our Lord, He chooses not to control every decision we make in life. I don't know about you but I really appreciate that. God could make everyone on the planet do exactly what He wants them to do but He chooses not to. We have a free will and we can use it to glorify Him through the choices we make with our lives.

I want to share some testimonies of how I pursued the will of God in my own life and how it has brought me closer to God. One example is the career path I decided to pursue after college. I was a psychology major and I thought that I wanted to be a psychologist. As time went on I realized it wasn't what I wanted to do. By the time my senior year came, I was stumped. I was looking into graduate schools in areas where I thought I would like to live and I started to make my own plan. Since I couldn't decide, I figured I would just go to the graduate school that gave me the most money.

Throughout this time I was mindful of God but I never truly sought His will. One day, I had a divine encounter with one of my professors as the Lord used her to speak to me. She told me that my method of making decisions was incorrect. She was a Christian and she told me that I needed to seek God's will for my life. She recommended that I go to the career center and take a career test as well. Although in my heart I knew I should seek God's will, I was afraid that He would make me do something I didn't want to do. After my conversation with my professor, I decided to actively seek the will of God for my life. I made the appointment, prayed and waited to hear from God.

Since I was making a major life decision, I also decided to fast. I really needed to hear from God and I wanted to make sure that I wasn't clouded by my own desires. I was choosing to pursue the will of God for my life. A few days before my appointment at the career center, God told me to take a career test on my own. I didn't go to any special website or pray for hours about it, I just typed in "career test" and clicked on the first link. After taking the test, the only result it gave was a teacher. I scrolled up and down looking for more options but there was only one. At that moment I knew it was God. Once I set in my heart to pursue the will of God for my life, everything fell into place. God led me to my next steps and I had a job before I graduated college.

I tell this testimony to show that God is interested in every detail of our lives. He is aware of what is going on with us but we have to be willing to listen to His guidance. He sees all and knows all. God created you and He knows what is best for you. So when you pursue His will for your life, you are setting yourself up to be fulfilled. God only wants what is good for you. There is no need to worry about your needs when you are in His will because He takes care of everything.

Another area where I have pursued the will of God was in my romantic relationships. Whomever I marry will have a huge impact on my life. I can't imagine making such a choice without God involved. I have witnessed the outcome of people who got married although it was clear it wasn't God's will for them to be together. Pain, heartache and divorce was the result of their choice.

I have had several opportunities to be in relationships with great men that wanted to get married. With each opportunity, I had a choice. A choice to make things happen my way or God's way. When there is a mutual connection with a person that you find attractive, it can be hard to put your desires to the side. I have found that each time that I have looked to the Lord to guide me in this area, He has been faithful. Answering my questions and showing me the truth.

In one instance, a man that I was very close to for many years decided that he wanted to be more than friends. We had a strong connection; our families knew each other and we had similar gifts and callings in ministry. It honestly made sense for us to be together. Although I was excited about the opportunity to be in a relationship, I didn't have peace. I couldn't pinpoint the error in my calculations but everything wasn't adding up. I knew that if I entered into this relationship without knowing God's will, I would regret it.

Once again, I prayed and fasted and sought the will of God. I asked Him to show me a vision of what my life would be like with this man. He showed me that although there would be fruit from our marriage and we could do a lot of ministry together, it ultimately wasn't the best choice for me. I was surprised by what I had been shown but felt extremely relieved by the clarity. I am so grateful that God gave me the wisdom I needed in that situation. I share this story to encourage you. God will give you wisdom when you ask. He doesn't want you to be unaware and unaligned. He wants you fully informed and attuned to His plan for your life.

While you are pursuing the will of God, it is vital that you do not open the door to the enemy by getting too many opinions. After I got clarification from God about what He wanted me to do, I talked with a leader in my life. He told me that I needed to continue to pray and ask God again because I might be wrong. Because I respected this person, I followed their advice but this confused me even more. Although I knew God spoke to me clearly about the issue, I began trusting in man's wisdom. There is a valuable lesson to be learned here. You have to learn how to hear from God yourself. You have to know when He is speaking to you. A sign of intimacy with God is trusting in what He says more than anyone else.

I have found that people stray from God's will because they don't trust His will. If you don't trust that the will of God for your life is best then you will try to make something happen in your own strength. Be careful that you do not go outside of God's will as a result of lacking trust in His timing and seeking to fill a void in your heart. Don't doubt His intentions and timing for you. Put your trust in Him like never before.

When we make our choices without His knowledge and wisdom, we open the door for the enemy. I encourage you to actively seek God's will. Proverbs 3:5-6 (NKJV) says "Trust in the Lord with all your heart, and lean not on your own understanding; in all your ways acknowledge Him and He shall direct your paths." In order for me to pursue the will of God and get the blessing, you have to trust Him.

To acknowledge God means we simply believe in God and yield to His way of doing things. The word acknowledge is a verb. It is an action word; it is something that we do. If you have not been actively pursuing the will of God for your life, I encourage you to start today. There is no time like the present to set your life on the path God has set for you.

You have to trust that what God has for you is the best option. No matter what it looks like, God knows what's best. We can't lean on our own understanding and what seems right. My life would be very different now if I had done things my way. Honestly, my life is nothing like I planned for myself years ago. I am extremely grateful for God's guidance.

In every area of your life begin to ask God, what do you desire? What is your best for me? What career do you want me to have? Where do you want me to live? Do you want me to continue this relationship? While you are single, learn to pursue God's will. Your time is precious and can be used wisely to pursue your purpose.

Many people desire to know what God wants them to do. 1 Corinthians 2:9 (NKJV) says "Eye has not seen, nor ear heard, nor have entered into the heart of man, the things which God has prepared for those who love Him." Every time I read this scripture I get excited. It reminds me that God has so many awesome things set up and ready for me to walk into. I don't have to think of it on my own or make it happen because God has prepared it for me.

The next verse says "But God has revealed them to us through His Spirit. For the Spirit searches all things, yes the deep things of God." (1 Cor. 2:10 NKJV) God reveals our purpose to us. By His Spirit, the things that He has planned for us are made known. Our gifts and talents and callings are made known. When we love God and actively pursue His will and the plan He has for our lives, He doesn't hide it from us.

Colossians 3:3 (NKJV) states "you have died and your life is hidden in Christ". Your life and your purpose are found when you pursue Christ. The more you get to know Him, the more you get to know yourself. You have an assignment to fulfill on this earth. There is a path that God has ordained for you to take. Pursue the will of God and He will reveal His plans to you.

Think about it...

- In what area of your life do you need to pursue the will of God?
- How can pursuing the will of God bring you closer to Him?
- What are the benefits of pursuing the will of God?

Prayer

God, I believe that you want what is best for me. I trust
you to lead me where I need to go. I desire to pursue
your will for me in every part of my life. I want you
involved and I want to be aligned with you. Help me
not to make plans without your wisdom and guidance.
May I be willing to yield to your desires for my life.

Chapter 9

Be Content

Contentment is a sign of stability and intimacy
in your relationship with Christ.

What is contentment? Is it easy to get or hard to find? Is it something that is available to some people while unimaginable or unattainable for others? One definition of contentment is being satisfied with what one is or has, not wanting more or anything else. How is that possible when we live in a society that always wants more and everything seems better than what we already have?

Contentment in God alone helps to guide your choices and decisions. Being content will help you to see clearly and keep you from becoming disillusioned. Single, godly, women that have God as their portion tend to keep themselves in alignment. Many poor relationship choices have been made by women who used marriage as a pill to relieve them of their discontentment. Sadly, they soon discover it wasn't the cure they were hoping for. Being content with being single can save you from unnecessary heartache and problems.

I believe that discontentment is one of the most prominent struggles single women face because most women are not truly satisfied in their singleness. Are you honestly okay with not being married? Do you feel fulfilled in your spirit, soul and body even though you're single? Contentment in singleness doesn't mean you don't desire marriage, it just means you are happy without it. In this chapter I will shed light on some of the reasons we find ourselves in a place of discontentment and ways that we can work through it.

I recall one night sitting on my bed talking to God and having no peace. I was really struggling with being single and I was weary. I went online to search for a sermon and stumbled upon a message about comparison and discontentment. It was the medicine I never knew I needed. After watching, I felt a freedom I hadn't felt in a long time. There was a shift. It was as if someone unchained me after years in a prison of discontentment ruled by the warden of comparison.

Comparison is often the cause of discontentment. It's so easy for women to compare themselves to others. We look at each other's hair, skin, body type, clothes, career, or finances and immediately begin comparing. Then afterwards we feel less than in comparison to the girl next to us. Comparison is a thief and we must treat it as such. It robs us of peace, joy and delight in our portion.

The enemy uses comparison to make us believe the lie that we are less than. For example, the more I looked at couples or stalked my ex on social media, the lonelier I felt. I compared what I saw on social media to my life and I always came up short. When I met a married woman, I would take note of her outward appearance and temperament. I then concluded that something in me was flawed or inadequate to justify why I was still single.

I believe that discontentment is also a posture of the heart. It's a lens through which you view your circumstances. If you feel unhappy with your position in life, it will spill over into every area. Discontentment tends to overshadow sunny dispositions. It leads to dwelling on the negative instead of the positive. Even when God has blessed you in many ways, discontentment can cause you to overlook those blessings and focus on the one thing you don't have.

Additionally, discontentment can come from having unrealistic expectations and putting God in a box. It's not wrong to have expectations, because that is a sign of our faith. However, it is wrong to make a plan in your mind and expect God to follow it. When that happens it puts a limit on what God can do in our lives.

For example, I used to go to church each Sunday thinking maybe today is the day I'm going to meet my husband. I would look around at who I thought it could be and try to put myself in situations where I would be noticed. By doing this, I was taking my attention off of God and setting myself up for disappointment. Although it didn't appear so on the outside, I would often leave service discouraged and dissatisfied. If I would have been more focused on meeting God and encountering Him in service, I would have gone further in my growth and development.

Overcoming discontentment in singleness starts in our minds. It begins with paying attention to our thoughts and choosing to believe the truth. There was a time where I constantly thought about being lonely. The more I thought about it, the wider I opened the door to self-pity and comparison and became extremely discontent in the process. I asked myself questions like, what's wrong with me? Why is everyone else getting married but me? When is it going to be my time? How much longer will I have to wait? These thoughts left me feeling powerless and defeated.

One day as I was thinking about how lonely I was and how sad I was being single and God spoke to my heart and said "Don't accept it." Then it finally hit me. My negative thoughts didn't originate from me. I was offered that thought and accepted it as truth. When we meditate on bad thoughts, they become exalted above God's truth and become more powerful than they should.

However, we have the power to cast down imaginations and every high thing that exalts itself against the knowledge of God and bring every thought captive to the obedience of Christ. (2 Corinthians 10:4-5 King James Version). God showed me that when I had a negative thought about being single, I needed to say something true out loud. I found scriptures that I could reference and sought to memorize them. And when I had a bad thought I could fight it with words like "God has plans to prosper me, to give me a hope and a future." (Jeremiah 29:11 NIV). The next time a crazy thought comes to your mind, speak the word of God out loud. Speak the truth out loud and those thoughts will flee.

Another piece of the puzzle came into play when God showed me that I was too focused on what I lacked. If you are struggling to find contentment in singleness, one key is to shift your focus from what you "lack". The truth is, you don't lack. As long as you seek the Lord you won't lack any good thing. That's scripture! Psalm 34:10 (NKJV) says "those who seek the LORD shall not lack any good thing."

I want to point out that this scripture says those who seek the Lord lack no good thing. If you are seeking marriage, or relationships, or any other thing besides God, then you will lack. Relationships were never designed to make us complete. Marriage was not designed to fulfill us. It is only when we seek God and become fulfilled in Him, that we find true happiness.

I know the pressures and fears that come along with being single. It can make you feel desperate and incomplete. But being single doesn't mean that you are incomplete. You are complete in God. If you don't feel complete in God alone, this must become a reality to you and your mindset must change. God wants you to be whole and complete in Him only. With God, you have all that you need.

I also had to realize that although I wanted a spouse, I didn't need one. That can sound harsh but it's the truth. Without a spouse, we are not half of a person. We are powerful individuals who find their complete satisfaction in God. Our source for life is in God alone. He is the only one that can truly satisfy us. Our greatest need will always be for more of God.

It's really all about perspective. 1 Corinthians 7:17 (The Message) says "don't be wishing you were someplace else or with someone else. Where you are right now is God's place for you. Live and obey and love and believe right there. God, not your marital status, defines your life." If you believe that your marital status defines your life, then you are going to be unhappy as a single. However, if you know that your life is defined by what God says, then you are free to be happy and content as a single person.

I've heard it said that singleness is an epidemic, especially in the church. It's true that when I look around after service there's more women than men. It's true that most of them are single. However, I don't believe God views it as a problem. God cares deeply for all of us and protects us. Viewing God as loving, protecting, kind and compassionate prevents us from thinking less of His intentions. I don't believe that God is allowing a widespread singleness epidemic. I believe He is sparing us from further hurt, pain and dysfunction.

I wonder how different the Church would be if it was filled with single people that were content with being single? I wonder what would be accomplished through women of God who walked in the fullness of their identity and happily waited on God to bring them a spouse? I wonder how many lives would be transformed by women who were at peace with their relationship status and found great pleasure in enjoying their relationship with Jesus? Let it start with you sis.

I know that learning how to be content during your season of singleness can be very difficult. The key is to find balance in this season and not spend too much time focusing on the past or the future. Allow God to show you His perspective on this season. Ask Him to help you not to see it as a burden, but a blessing. Your life is a gift from God. He wants you to enjoy it. Live everyday of your life in celebration of the gift He has given you.

Take some time to think about how you define life and happiness. Do you think you have to be married to be happy? Do you think you have to be in a relationship to be happy? Do you believe that you can be content as a single person? God desires for you to be happy and at peace with being single. He doesn't want you to rush out of this season or stray from His will because you are unhappy. Decide today that you will no longer be discontent being single.

In Psalm 37:3 (NKJV), the second part of the verse says, "Dwell in the land and feed on His faithfulness." This means to stay where you are and be content. Don't be hasty or make something happen on your own. Think about His faithfulness and all He has done for you. When you are lonely, questioning God and hungering for a relationship, feed on, think about and meditate on how faithful He has been to you.

Another way to combat discontentment is to develop a habit of thankfulness. Spend time in the morning meditating on all the ways God has blessed you. Begin to record all the things He has done for you and document these things as they happen. I have a testimony journal where I write down things God does for me, no matter how big or small. Write down what God does for you and all the ways He shows himself faithful to you. By doing this you will be cultivating a grateful heart which is the spiritual antidote for discontentment.

God never intended for marriage to be a stumbling block. He never intended for it to be an idol. However, He did intend for us to live abundant lives (John 10:10 NKJV). It's difficult to live an abundant life if you are distracted by finding a mate. Find your contentment in knowing that God knows right where you are in life. He knows your struggles and desires. He knows everything about you and intends for you to live a good life.

Contentment is all about rest. Contentment is demonstrated when you are humble enough to wait on the Lord and trust in Him to bring it to pass instead of being prideful and making things happen your own way. Contentment is a sign of stability and intimacy in your relationship with Christ. Even when it's difficult to hold on, believe that you can do all things through Christ who strengthens you. (Philippians 4:13 NKJV). Learn how to be content in whatever state you are in.

I didn't settle into contentment overnight and there are definitely still days where I struggle. It typically comes about when I focus on being in a relationship with a man and not with God. However, one thing that has kept me grounded is allowing Jesus to be enough for me. The largest pearl of wisdom I've received about being single, came from a woman who spoke at a conference I went to. Sadly, I don't remember her name but her words have never left me.

In her message, she spoke about things that women should do to prepare themselves for marriage and she ended with a simple phrase. "Pray that in the secret place of your heart, Jesus will always be enough." These words stopped time and pierced me deeply. At that point in my life, I couldn't say that Jesus was enough for me. I wanted a relationship more than anything else. So, when she said those words, I knew that God was speaking to me.

For years, I have treasured that phrase. It's kept me anchored season after season. When I'm on the edge and seriously struggling with being single, I remind myself that Jesus is enough for me. If I never get married, Jesus is enough. Jesus has to be enough for us all. No matter what happens in life, we have to be settled in the reality that He is our portion. Discontentment is unfruitful and I hope I have shed light on ways to dispel it.

Think about it...

- Would you still be happy with your life if you never got married?
- How has God been faithful to you?
- What would it take for you to be content with being single?

Here are a few things to confess or speak out loud when negative thoughts about being single come to your mind:

- I seek the Lord and I don't lack any good thing (Psalm 34:10)
- I will delight myself in the Lord and He will give me the desires of my heart (Psalm 37:4)
- I will rest in the Lord, and wait patiently for Him (Psalm 37:7)
- God will keep me in perfect peace because I trust in Him and my thoughts are fixed on Him (Isaiah 26:3)

- God is always faithful to me
- I will not live in disappointment
- In the secret place of my heart, Jesus will always be enough for me

Prayer

Lord, I pray for grace to find contentment in my singleness. You know my desires and I choose to commit them to you. Help me not to focus on what I lack. Help me to divert my thoughts to all the good you have blessed me with when I feel discouraged. Please help me to see the benefits of this season. Show me how I can delight in you and help me to trust you with my future. May I have peace in my soul regardless of my marital status. I pray that in the secret place of my heart, you will always be enough for me.

Chapter 10

Trust God and Surrender

With trust comes deeper communion.

I felt that I needed to add this chapter because of my experiences over the years since I wrote this book. Seven years have gone by and I've lived more life. I'm currently 32 and I'm not married or dating anyone. In my early 20's, I had an expectation for the way my life would turn out. I thought I would be married, have several children and a house by this age. I thought I would live somewhere else and have a different career than I currently do. But God had other plans.

When I wrote this book in 2014, I thought that my devotion and strict obedience to the Lord would grant me quicker access to a husband and family. Somehow, I thought that my actions would put me on the fast track to marriage. There was a part of me that believed marriage was the ultimate goal. The shiny trophy, waiting for me at the end of the finish line. I worked hard to be a good Christian girl. So, surely God would reward me by giving me what I wanted, when I wanted.

Unfortunately, I didn't realize that I was idolizing marriage. I was looking to marriage to deliver me from loneliness and as the answer to many of my problems. I didn't see the ways that I had been lured away from the truth because I let my desire for marriage supersede my desire for God. The more that I focused on my desire for marriage the easier it became to compromise on what I believed was God's best for my life. Over time, I became discontent because Jesus wasn't truly enough for me.

My desires distracted me from running my race. My eyes were not fixed on the author and finisher of my faith. Hebrews 12:1 (NKJV) says "let us lay aside every weight and the sin which so easily ensnares us, and let us run with endurance the race that is set before us." For me, worrying about marriage was a weight. I was more concerned about getting married than being with God and fulfilling my purpose. I was not free to run the race set before me because I was tangled in my thoughts about marriage.

I know many of you may find yourself in a similar circumstance. Your life may not look the way you planned. You might want something that seems unattainable at the moment and it's frustrating. You may feel powerless and out of control because you have no ability to make what you want happen. Or you may even find yourself in a situation where you are settling just so you can have a measure of what you truly desire. Many single women worry if they will ever get married and what their future will hold. Many struggle to yield their hopes for a relationship in faith that God will bring it to pass at the right time. Some even hold themselves back and play it safe because they are waiting for a spouse.

I wrote this chapter because I know how difficult it can be to trust God. I know that surrendering a desire to Him is hard. I've had to surrender my desire for marriage to Him over and over again. I've had to say no to relationships I wanted to say yes to. I've had to have faith that He is faithful and trustworthy. I've had to let go of my expectations and relinquish control.

Trusting God with your relationship status and surrendering to His timing can be tough. At times it has seemed that as I've increased in age, I have decreased in patience and understanding. I really struggled during a season when several of my friends started to get married. I truly felt overlooked and forgotten by God. I felt desperate and sad because marriage seemed to happen naturally for others but I could barely get a date. There were many times when I wanted to take matters into my own hands and not wait on God.

Surrendering my desire for marriage has not been easy. I've been angry with God and questioned His love for me. I've been frustrated with His timing. I've been disobedient and stayed in situations with guys that He told me to let go of. I've had my share of meltdowns and cried myself to sleep many nights. I've been cynical and bitter to the point of pessimism. Uncertain that God would actually deliver what He promised. But through it all, I let myself feel the emotions and brought them to God. My journey hasn't been perfect but I still choose to trust God.

I believe that learning to trust God at a deeper level is one of the greatest benefits of being single. We are all on a journey with the Lord and we learn to trust Him more in every season of life. However, there is something special about being able to develop a foundation of trust in the Lord as a single person. There is nothing like hearing Him for yourself, taking a risk and seeing God meet you on the other side. As you allow God to show Himself faithful to you, it builds confidence and intimacy in your relationship with Him.

With trust comes deeper communion. The more you trust someone, the closer you become to them. If you constantly fear that your needs won't be met or that you will get hurt, then it can be difficult to reach a place of true intimacy. Most of the time, a lack of trust springs from unbelief and doubt in God. We don't believe that He will come through the way we want Him to. We doubt that He will do what He promised. As a single person, take your time to deal with the belief systems that hinder your ability to trust God.

I was hindered by a fear of disappointment. I couldn't put the full weight of my trust in Him. I was terrified to rely on Him for something meaningful. It was easier to believe that God would let me down than believe that He would satisfy me. Doubt came easily when I dwelled on situations where I had been let down in the past. I was afraid to trust God with the things I cared about deeply.

This fear presented itself in subtle ways. For example, there was a period of time when I found all the men that were interested in me unattractive. They were great guys but I had no chemistry with them. It was happening so much that I started to make up an explanation in my head. I concluded that God was going to make me settle for someone that I wasn't attracted to. I've heard many single women utter the same concern. This fear revealed what was really in my heart. I didn't trust Him or know Him well enough. I didn't believe that God was really good.

The more we know about God and His character, the more our trust in Him increases. The bible says in James 1:17 (NKJV) "Every good gift and every perfect gift is from above, and comes down from the Father of lights, with whom there is no variation or shadow of turning." Here we can clearly see that God is good and constant. This motivates us to trust Him. Everything good that we have comes from Him, so there is no need to fear that our needs won't be met and that we will end up disappointed.

Surrendering our timelines and dreams to God can only happen when we trust Him. Surrender is laying down our power and ability to get what we want in order to receive what God wants for us at the proper time. It requires faith to believe that what God has for us is best and that He will bring it at the right time. Think about what happened with Abraham and Sarah. They took matters into their own hands in order to get what they wanted and ended up with problems and heartache. (Genesis 16, 21)

Trusting God keeps you safe from making decisions that you might regret. It is far better to depend on God than do things your own way. Don't be hasty but rather wait. Lay down your power and ability to bring things to pass and allow God to bring it at the right time. Let God be the author of your story.

Many years ago, I was head over heels for a guy at my church. I thought for sure that he was my husband. He was a youth pastor, attractive, smart, funny and the list goes on. All my friends would tell me how good we looked together and that we would be a perfect match. I even had what I thought were "confirmations" or signs from God that He was my husband but we never made it past a few dates. Sometime later, he began dating someone else and I was completely devastated. He was supposed to be my husband. How could he possibly be dating someone else?

I was so upset with God because I truly believed that he was supposed to be with me. I've heard many women share similar occurrences. They thought that God was speaking to them about being in a relationship with a person only to be disappointed later down the line. It's confusing and discouraging when we believe that we heard God leading us in one direction only to find it leads to a dead end. Especially when it's something that we really want.

After I shed my tears and avoided God for a while, I decided to open myself back up to hear from Him. I was honest about my feelings and prayed for clarity. He showed me that I needed to trust that He wouldn't lead me down the wrong path. I needed to believe that He knew who was best for me. I couldn't see clearly then but now I thank God I'm not married to that man. We weren't truly compatible and in hindsight, I realize that I was more intrigued by all of the roles he played in church then who he was as a person.

God also told me that all the signs I received about him being my husband stemmed from my own reasoning. I took all his actions so seriously and tried to make sense of everything on my own without God. Even if he was truly interested in me, that didn't mean that we were supposed to get married. I was seeing things my way, trying to make it be something that it wasn't. I was so clouded by my thoughts of being in a relationship, that I wasn't truly open to hear from God. I wanted God to do things my way instead of the other way around.

Trusting God and surrendering to Him will occur after a revelation of His timelessness. God has been, is and will be. He was in our past, is in our present and will be in our future. Since He can see the whole picture it's best to let Him lead. He knows exactly how to get us to our destinations. It's up to us to limit the number of detours we take on the way.

I had to humble myself and realize that when I gave my life to Christ I chose not to be in control. It's no longer about what I want. As a follower of Jesus I made the decision to give up my rights and trust Him to lead me where He wants me to go. I may want to get married but God may have other plans. If marriage is not in the plan then I have to trust that God knows what He is doing and find peace without it. It's a tension that I must wrestle with. I have hope and faith that I will get married but I trust God and surrender my will to Him. I look to Him to satisfy me above all else.

Sometimes in life, things don't go our way. Our situations do go according to plan and it can be very upsetting. We can find comfort in knowing that God's ways are higher and better than we could imagine. Isaiah 55:8-9 (NLT) says "My thoughts are nothing like your thoughts," says the Lord. "And my ways are far beyond anything you could imagine. For just as the heavens are higher than the earth, so my ways are higher than your ways and my thoughts higher than your thoughts." Knowing this truth will help us to surrender to God even when we don't understand.

Jesus is the ultimate example of what it looks like to trust God and surrender to Him. This is what Paul wrote of Jesus in Philippians 2:5-8 (NLT) "You must have the same attitude that Christ Jesus had. Though he was God, he did not think of equality with God as something to cling to. Instead, he gave up his divine privileges; he took the humble position of a slave and was born as a human being. When he appeared in human form, he humbled himself in obedience to God and died a criminal's death on a cross."

Jesus had every right to be entitled. He is the Son of God and could have done much with His freedom and power. However, He submitted Himself to the Father and gave up His life. He let go of His divinity. He let go of His power. In Luke 22:42 (NLT) Jesus said "Father, if you are willing, please take this cup of suffering away from me. Yet I want your will to be done, not mine." Jesus let go of what He wanted in order to pursue God's will. He trusted that God the Father's way was the best way.

As His followers, we must do the same. We have to trust that He is good and that His plan and purpose for us is good no matter what. We can't let our doubts and fears cloud what we know to be true of His character. We must give up our right to understand and look to the one who is higher. On our journey to become more intimate with God, we will have to trust and surrender repeatedly. If Jesus did it, then we can too.

My prayer is that we trust God and surrender to Him. May we be people who relinquish control and let Him have His way in our lives. I pray that you would be focused, submitted to God and free to run your race without distraction. I pray that you would learn to trust God completely and hold nothing back from Him. May you experience the peace that comes with trusting God with your story.

God doesn't just want you to benefit from an intimate relationship with Him, He wants your family, your children, co-workers and everyone you encounter to benefit from the intimacy you have. This book is about more than what to do while you wait for a husband. This book is about having a real relationship with Jesus. It's about letting God take control of your life so that He can use you. It's about knowing how much He loves you and wants to be with you. However, the level of intimacy you experience with God will come as a result of how much you yield your life to Him. Be open to what God wants to do in your life and work with Him to see it come to pass.

Think about it...

- How comfortable are you with letting God have full control of your life?
- Are there any reasons why you don't believe God is good?
- How does knowing that God is timeless help you to trust Him?

Prayer

Father, I surrender all of myself to you because you are good and perfect. You know and see it all. Thank you for being safe for me to put my hope and trust in. God I pray that you will help me to surrender any area that I am withholding. I relinquish control to you. Thank you for caring about every detail of my life and working everything together in your perfect timing. Please give me grace to stay strong and not compromise. Help me not to be impatient. Please give me hope and peace as I wait on you to bring my dreams to fruition.

References

"Scripture quotations taken from the Amplified® Bible
Copyright © 1954, 1958, 1962, 1964, 1965,
1987 by The Lockman Foundation
Used by permission." (www.Lockman.org)

Copyright © 2006 by World Bible Translation Center

"Scripture taken from *The Message*. Copyright ©
1993, 1994, 1995, 1996, 2000, 2001, 2002. Used
by permission of NavPress Publishing Group."

THE HOLY BIBLE, NEW INTERNATIONAL
VERSION®, NIV® Copyright © 1973,
1978, 1984, 2011 by Biblica, Inc.® Used by
permission. All rights reserved worldwide.

Scripture taken from the New King James
Version®. Copyright © 1982 by Thomas Nelson.
Used by permission. All rights reserved

Scripture quotations marked (NLT) are taken from
the Holy Bible, New Living Translation, copyright
© 1996, 2004, 2007 by Tyndale House Foundation.
Used by permission of Tyndale House Publishers, Inc.,
Carol Stream, Illinois 60188. All rights reserved.

About the Author

Deja Smith lives in Maryland and attends Victory Christian Ministries International. She is passionate about seeing the body of Christ developing intimacy with Jesus. Deja is a leader, teacher, and singer/songwriter. She is a devoted follower of Jesus and a light to the body of Christ.

Printed in the United States
by Baker & Taylor Publisher Services